49

KEEP THIS
KITCHEN
CLEAN & TIDY

101 ESSENTIAL TIPS

FOR RUNNING A *PROFESSIONAL* HMO

GIVING YOU TIME, MONEY AND FREEDOM!

WENDY WHITTAKER-LARGE

Published by Centre Round Publishing
www.centreround.com

A catalogue record for this book is available from the British Library

ISBN 978-1-513607-32-0

Printed and bound in the UK

First edition 2015

Second edition 2020

For Mark and Gavin

Wendy Whittaker-Large,

is the founder of multiple companies including Best Nest – a high end HMO company – and HMO Success – an HMO training company. She is passionate about HMOs for their contribution to the housing economy and the positive contribution they can make to people's lives. Over the last 18 years she has steadily built a multi-million pound property portfolio whilst raising a family and running an award-winning business. She now helps other people to achieve financial freedom whilst juggling domestic and family commitments, enabling them to fulfil their dreams of having a much higher quality of life and more time to spend with their children and family. She works with a whole range of people – from those with young families and full-time jobs to older people looking to secure their financial future for retirement.

Her passion is to help others find freedom by creating long-term residual income. If that's what you want, please get in touch by visiting **www.wendywl.uk**

TIP FINDING IT
1. Macro location
2. Micro location
3. Estate agents
4. Below Market Value
5. Trading Denominations
6. Head and Heart
7. Leveraging Size
8. Property Footprint
9. Space
10. Bikes
11. Property Frontage
12. Conversions
13. Planning

TIP FUNDING IT
14. How to fund it
15. Local market conditions
16. Survey Information
17. Paperwork
18. Empty homes grants
19. Protect the downsides
20. Predictions
21. ROI
22. Creating Infinite ROI
23. Working with Investors
24. Key Performance Indicators
25. Photos and Videos
26. Your Valuation Pack
27. Working with a Mortgage Advisor
28. Becoming a Fascination for Financiers!

TIP FINISHING IT
29. Your Power Team
30. Plans
31. Specification
32. Using your Survey
33. Day of Completion
34. Keylock
35. Scoping the Project
36. Discounts
37. VAT
38. Power Sockets & Lighting
39. Energy Efficiency
40. Tiling
41. Taking Advice
42. Project Planning
43. Roles and Responsibilities
44. Phases
45. Stage Payments
46. Choices
47. Broadband
48. Masterkey
49. Snagging
50. Colour Schemes
51. Co-ordination
52. Furniture
53. Storage Space
54. Floor Coverings
55. Appliances
56. Cleaning
57. Exterior

TIP FILLING IT
58. Preparation
59. Dressing
60. Noticeboards and Signage
61. Crib Sheets
62. Setting the Rent
63. Photographs
64. Create your Advert
65. Advertising Online
66. Using Social Media
67. Prospective Tenant Information
68. Requests for Viewings
69. Block Bookings

70. Viewings
71. The Letting Process
72. Securing your Fee
73. Working Smartly
74. Undertaking References
75. Collecting Deposit and Initial Rent
76. Moving-In
77. Induction
78. Practicalities
79. Introductions
80. Courtesy Call

TIP FUTURE-PROOFING IT
81. Customer Service
82. Communication
83. Check-out Process
84. Returning the Deposit
85. Evicting Bad Tenants
86. Re-advertising
87. Incentivise Tenants
88. Bins
89. Lead Responsible Tenant
90. Tenant Communication Systems
91. Keys
92. Other Systems
93. Maintenance
94. Tradespeople
95. Tenant Lock-Outs
96. Legislation & Accreditation
97. Maximise your Rent
98. Rent Collection
99. Outgoings
100. Technology
101. Enjoy It!

The book is split into five sections:

FIND IT, FUND IT, FINISH IT, FILL IT and FUTURE-PROOF IT

Each section contains tips that are large and in-depth or are short and sweet. ALL of the advice will be useful if you are developing for the young professional HMO market and could save you thousands of pounds and hours of worry. **Giving you time, money and freedom as a result.**

INTRODUCTION

Whether you are brand new to HMOs or know the ropes like a true professional, this book will help you FIND, FUND, FINISH, FILL and FUTURE-PROOF your investment.

The tips here have been gleaned from my work over the last few years in building a profitable, high-yielding and great cash-flowing HMO portfolio. When I started out in HMOs I really knew almost nothing about the industry. I was truly wet behind the ears and had to learn everything from scratch. I got my hands dirty in the nuts and bolts of the process, including learning about building regulations and all the amendments, drilling down into legislation and policy to ensure the portfolio I was creating met all the standards and exceeded them in some instances, and of course applying the practical day-to-day knowledge that I have developed, refined and tested. Although many investors desire to get into the HMO market, HMOs require more skills and knowledge than single lets due to the complexities that they can present. There are more complex issues to be faced such as planning, building regulations and licensing. Financing too can be tricky and expensive if you don't plan ahead. Many agents don't manage HMOs so finding a good one can be hard, unless you want to deal with the tenants personally.

So I have written this book as a handy guide to helping you quickly and efficiently learn some tricks of the trade and apply them in your

chosen HMO location. All the tips in the book have been implemented, tested and refined in my company, Best Nest. They will enable you to create a well-managed, profitable professional HMO and also free up your time. By implementing the knowledge in this book you will be able to create a systemised business that runs even when you're not there. This book is focused on the professional HMO market, but many of the pieces of advice can easily be applied to other sectors of the market such as LHA (local housing allowance) and student HMOs.

The book is split into five sections:

FIND IT, FUND IT, FINISH IT, FILL IT and FUTURE-PROOF IT

Each section contains tips large and small – some you may already be aware of (yet worth being reminded of) and some slightly longer and in-depth. I know I stand on the shoulder of giants – others who have inspired me to grow my HMO business and created amazing HMO businesses themselves. In so doing they have become remarkable people and have the lifestyle and the ability to give back to others as a result of their work. If I inspire you, challenge you, inform you, educate you or entertain you, please let me know! I would be delighted to hear your stories and how I can help you further.

Wendy Whittaker Large

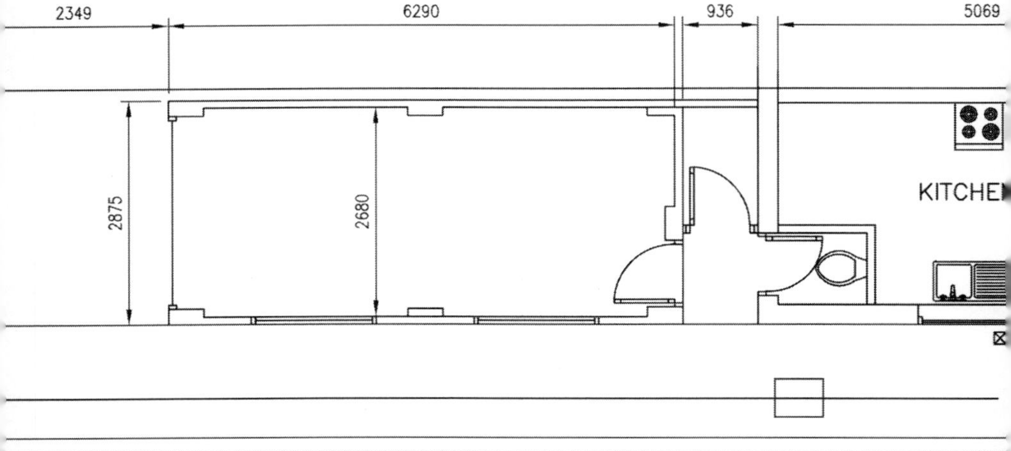

EXISTING GROUND FLOOR

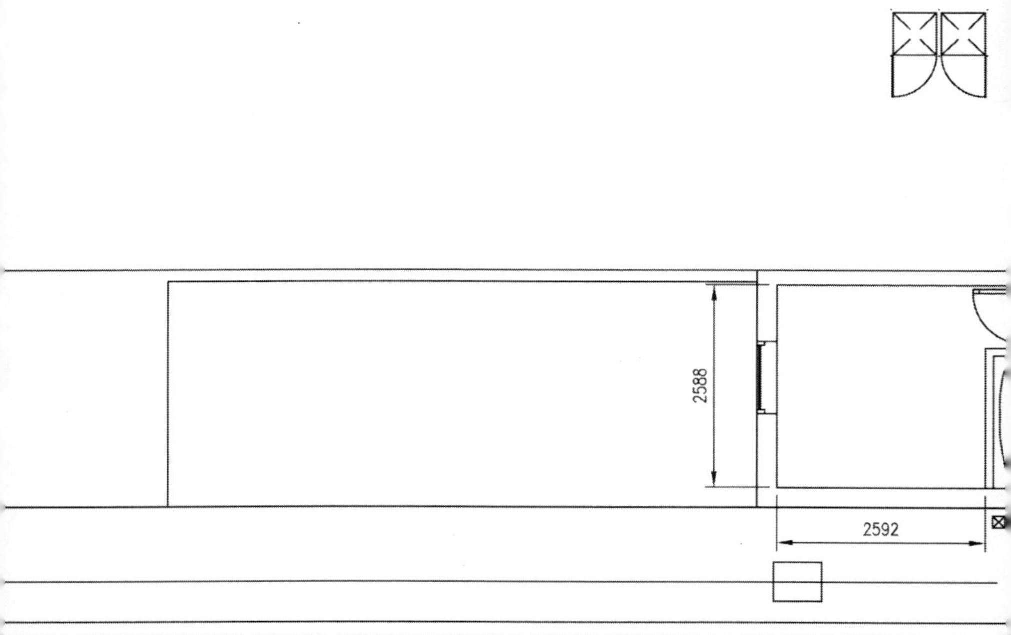

EXISTING FIRST FLOOR

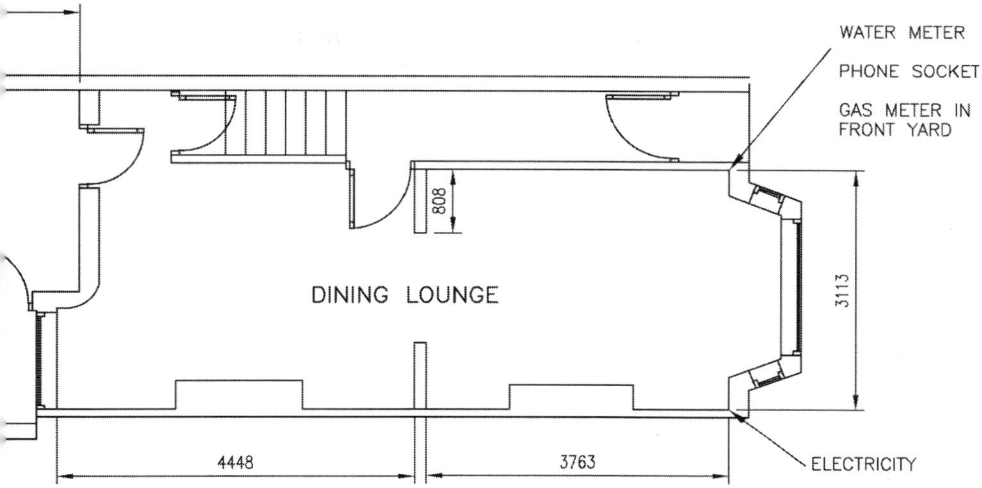
WATER METER
PHONE SOCKET
GAS METER IN FRONT YARD
808
DINING LOUNGE
3113
ELECTRICITY
4448
3763

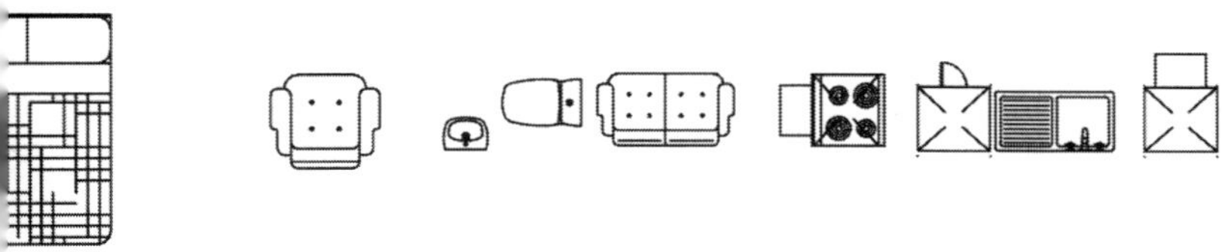

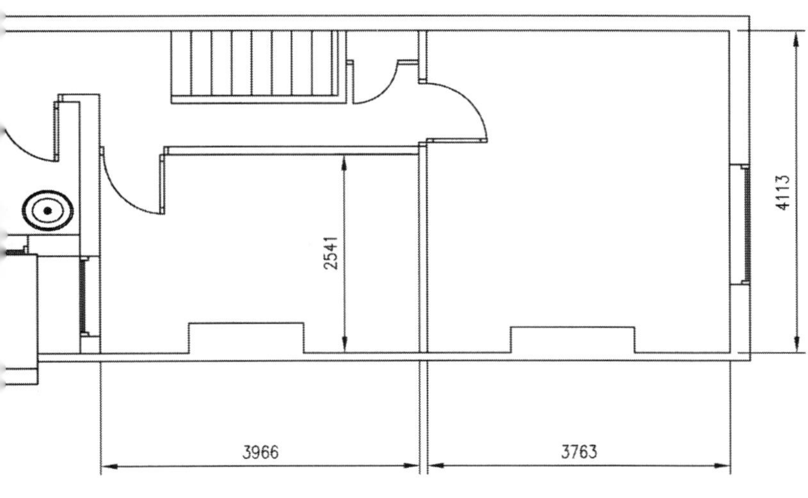
4113
2541
3966
3763

FINDING IT

Finding the right location for your HMO might take some time but if you want to create an HMO that cashflows for many years to come, your due diligence now is worth it.

This is the first step in the process and the MOST important. Identifying your ideal investment area will also allow you to grow your portfolio quickly as you test and refine your model with a relatively small set of variables. This will eventually save you time and money and allow you to create a 'cookie-cutter' approach and repeat the same steps faster and more efficiently each time.

Initially you will need to choose your 'macro' location. This is the town or city where you are going to make a professional HMO work for you. In terms of an area where the most successful professional HMOs are located, there are some key characteristics you need to look for, which are namely:

- A population of NO LESS than 80,000 people – otherwise you are unlikely to have the right number and supply of houses
- Robust and various transport links to the wider region (train, coach, bus, motorway, tram etc)
- Within 20 miles of another equally large conurbation
- At least 10 medium to large employers (1000 people plus) who have a significant need for skilled or semi-skilled labour
- Local plans for growth, regeneration and investment (this is not always easy to uncover but looking at the local plan will ascertain local trends for housing and employment. Knowing the priorities of your local council for development over the next five years is a core part of understanding the viability of a potential HMO)
- Retail and shopping facilities that cater for all segments of the population
- At least 10–15% of property in the rental market (i.e. predictable and steady rental market). This is true of most of the UK at present! This factor is important as it influences your tenants' ability to move up and out of your HMO eventually. Some may leave due to job changes, others will purchase their own property and many will move into a single let property. If there is limited opportunity to move up the rental ladder this will affect the popularity of the area with regard to HMO room lets. Also having a strong local rental demand will ensure there are plenty of lettings agents locally who you can work with to let out rooms

tip2

Next you need to choose your 'micro' location – namely the subdivisions of the 'macro' area which will be suitable as a location for an HMO. In terms of a micro area the local characteristics to look for are as follows:

- Local, corner shop-type facilities within 1–2 streets away OR large supermarket nearby
- Some entertainment facilities (cinema, bowling, theatre) within a couple of miles of your proposed HMO
- Health centres and/or GP facilities within 2 miles and a large hospital within 15 miles
- Public transport facilities such as bus routes or trams or trains within a few streets (15–20 min walk maximum)
- AVOID double yellow lines outside a property if you can. Not only will this inhibit the tenants to park nearby to the property if they need to, it also indicates a busy road which may deter them
- AVOID buying in an Article 4 area if possible (see appendix for more details of this legislation)

Don't be put off if you can't tick off all these indicators in your chosen location, but be aware that tenants need access to practical services and may not always have a car, so local services are much more important.

When trying to find your ideal macro or micro location, talk to the local estate agents.

By tapping into their local knowledge and understanding their 'take' on the market, you will make them feel that they are indispensable to you. That is a nice feeling to have, and will usually make them more motivated to help you. However, remember that their service exists for a reason — to make money, and therefore any time you spend with them needs to be efficient and organised. Being clear with agents about what you want from the outset helps them and it helps you. Even if you only want 1 HMO in a particular area, let them think that you are a long term serious investor who wants to build a portfolio. Be clear about your micro area. It is true for estate agents as it is for any other commercial enterprise — it costs 10 times more to find a new customer than to sell to a current one. By intimating that you may buy more than one property, you will motivate them to ensure you are contacted with properties that match your search criteria. (And depending on how your first investment works out, indeed you might end up being a prolific local investor).

bonus tip

Like many sellers, agents want speed and certainty.

tip4

BMV refers to **Below Market Value** and is a certainly a preferable price to pay for a property!

Your due diligence and research will confirm the market size, position and trends of property in your 'macro and micro' area and will allow you to determine confidently what the market price is of a property. Owning other properties in a specific area (or knowing other landlords who do) is a useful tool to judge current prices as is previous recent sales information (which can be found on www.zoopla.com and www.landregistry.gov.uk).

tip5

If you find a property by working direct with a vendor, always remember that money is not the only trade denomination available to you. You may have time, knowledge or contacts that you can leverage to influence the decision of a vendor.

tip6

Never become emotionally attached to the purchase — let your head rule your heart at all times. There will ALWAYS be another deal around the corner. If you lose this one, don't fret — move on and keep looking.

extra tip

A useful website which delves deeper into the local sales statistics and offers insight into your local area is www.home.co.uk. You can search the volumes and numbers of local estate agents sales and identify the ones who are selling houses faster and for more money.

---

tip7

Leveraging the full size of the property to create additional income-producing rooms creates the flexibility of pricing which you may need should the market change, and gives a good cushion against voids. If you don't have good spatial awareness or 3-dimensional vision, take someone with you to view your potential HMO who does. Someone else might be able to see how space can be used creatively to increase real or perceived value. If you can find a builder who can do this, so much the better as he or she can also estimate a price for the conversion there and then (although be aware this is only a ROUGH ESTIMATE at this stage. A more detailed assessment comes later).

tip8

Calculate the footprint of the overall property. There needs to be some outside space for relaxation, a place for a table and chairs to sit out in the summer, and perhaps a barbecue (ensure you put up fire safety notices)! Space for a rotary airer, and at least 3 bins is also needed. These are usually a main waste bin, a recycling bin and a garden waste bin as a minimum. If the garden is fully hard standing you can ask for the council to replace this with another recycling bin. You can usually ask for additional bins from the council too depending on the size of your HMO.

tip9

Space and sizing. Minimum room sizes for licensed HMOs were introduced in 2018. Therefore, if your property will have five or more tenants from two or more households each room should meet the minimum legal standards of 10m2 for a double room and 6.52m2 for a single room. When assessing a property for size, attic rooms need to be measured carefully as do cellars for potential bedrooms. Floor area can only be counted where the head height is at least 1.5m. Therefore a house which has an attic room that could be converted can be used as long as the room size of 10m2 can be achieved if the head height of that 10m2 is 1.5m. The same applies to cellar spaces. These can be converted into bedrooms, but in this case exit passages and access to light are considerations. A large enough dining kitchen area needs to be provided and there may be other amenity standards that your local council has passed. Check your local council guidelines which will specify the details.

tip 10

Bikes! Many HMO tenants will use a bike as their main form of transport – so you must consider where they can be left safely and securely. The hallway of the house is not a suitable location for a bike! Not only does it create a safety hazard it is against fire regulations. In some areas, and where you need planning permission there is a requirement for cycle racks to be installed. So consider access to the rear of the property for tenants to be able to bring bikes in, and also to move bins in and out.

tip 11

The front of the property ideally must not sit right on the pavement. Otherwise this tends to severely limit the 'rentability' of the front downstairs bedroom. A small front yard area or garden, with a hedge or fence allows some privacy to the front of the house, and makes the downstairs bedroom far easier to rent. If there is a parking space or a parking area adjacent to or in front of the property this is a great additional bonus. Remember to highlight this in the advertising. Double yellow lines outside a property can be a sign that this might not be in an ideal location.

tip 12

Commercial properties can make ideal conversions into HMOs as often they are situated in or around a town or city centre, have large rooms and services already provided. Permitted development rights allow you to change certain commercial properties into residential accommodation. Your local planning officer will guide you through what is allowable and what is not. If you are considering a large conversion, it's a good idea to utilise the services of a local planning consultant – they know the rules and guidance and will carefully guide you through the process. The permitted development rights will only cover change of use: any associated physical development which currently requires a planning application will continue to need one.

Remember to check the planning guidance from the local council if you are planning on

a. Creating a 7 bed or more HMO (when you will need 'sui generis' planning)

b. In an Article 4 area (where there are restrictions on planning for HMOs

c. Extending or otherwise changing the property externally

Once you have found your 'ideal' property to convert into an HMO – whether that be a 'small HMO' which is 5 beds or less, a medium 6 bed or a large 7 bed or more, your next steps will be determined by how you **Fund It.**

bonus tip

Some people love it, some people loathe it but networking with other property investors who own HMOs should be a priority at this early stage. Networking allows you to meet other people who have trodden the path before you so that you can tap into what they have learnt. As they share their learning and experiences you will find that there are many 'models' even of professional HMOs –

a. Exclusive / Luxury HMOs
b. Bijou HMOs
c. Basic HMOs
d. Foreign friendship group HMOs
e. Mini Mo HMOs (4 rooms or less)

You will design your HMO around the location of the property, the local tenant market, your budget and your competition. Your own preferences should be last on the list! There's no point designing a basic HMO in an area where every other HMO is a luxury one unless you know it is a sector of the market where there is demand and little supply. That is why networking is so important as it allows you to meet the investors who are also in the market and understand their strategies and insight into the local area.

FUNDING IT

The market for funding HMOs is constantly changing. Staying abreast of changes in the mortgage market is critical if you are to get the best deal from your broker or financier.

Always find a reputable broker who understands HMO financing and has experience in the market place, and who can help package your HMO effectively and thus get the best deal. However even in this fluctuating market there are ways to ensure that you get the very best valuation and thus offer from your mortgage provider. You may wish to work with another investor or individual who has money but no time or experience, in a Joint Venture. These can be very profitable for both parties, but they too take time and consideration to work properly.

tip 14

Firstly you must decide how you want to fund your HMO. Source a financial advisor who has experience and expertise in financing HMOs. Don't just use a high street mortgage advisor. HMOs are unique, semi-commercial operations (especially if they are licensed and in an Article 4 area) so you need to work with someone who has experience in this area and can advise you effectively. Some questions to consider :

- Will you use your own cash for the deposit and get a mortgage immediately?
- How will you fund the refurbishment or building costs?
- Will you fund the whole development with cash?
- Will you be re-financing when the project is finished?
- Will you use another investor's money for all or part of it?
- If so, what is the repayment period, the interest rate, or the agreement with the JV (joint venture) partner?

When working with JV partners it is imperative that you stay on the right side of the law and protect the interests of your partner and yourself from the beginning. New financial regulations (PS 13–03) were introduced in the UK in 2013 which you need to be familiar with before creating a Joint Venture or investment opportunity (www.fca.org.uk).

tip 15

If you haven't already done this, now is the time to consider fully the local market conditions. How much are other rooms being rented for in the area? (check spareroom.co.uk, easyroommate.co.uk and rightmove.co.uk for comparables). What is the condition and décor of these comparable properties like? How will you differentiate your HMO from the competition? Are there ways you can increase your rents without a massive cost outlay? Ensure you plan in any additional features or benefits to the HMO early on so that you can budget for them too.

tip 16

If you have had a survey undertaken either for mortgage purposes, or for your own information, use this as a starting point for assessing the structural fabric of the property and the financial outlay necessary. This includes the roof, windows and doors, walls and floors. It may be necessary to glean advice from a specialist tradesman (or woman) regarding the quality of these areas before deciding whether to replace, repair or simply revamp them. Unless you are an experienced property developer or builder it is easy to miss problems even after a couple of viewings. Things like a flying freehold, boundary issues, or single brick extensions (common in Victorian buildings) may make it harder to re-finance the property later on. So ensure that you utilise specialists throughout the process to avoid problems later on. And remember, most problems can be rectified in property. Yes it may take longer and cost more, but that shouldn't necessarily dissuade you, as these issues can become useful negotiation tools with the price.

tip 17

And speaking of negotiation tools, read all the paperwork you receive from your solicitor thoroughly before purchase. It was only when we received the vendor's pack from our solicitor regarding a property we were purchasing to convert into a 6 bed HMO that we noticed the box had been ticked where the vendor was asked the question 'Are you aware of any occurrence of Japanese Knotweed in or around the property?'! This had not previously been disclosed, so it was only through reading the paperwork thoroughly that we picked this up. As a result we renegotiated the price to cover the cost of the work (£6000) that was needed!

tip 18

Claim all the empty homes grants and amounts you can – contact the local council to understand what their criteria are – often you may find loans, grants and other benefits are open to you if you are buying a home that has been empty for a while.

tip 19

A good investor protects against the downsides. Therefore any property that meets your requirement for an HMO ideally needs to have the flexibility to be converted back into a residential property or another use of property should the worst occur, and it not be possible to utilise it as an HMO any longer. (Even if that includes undertaking a planning reversion).

tip 20

> ## bonus tip
>
> Always plan in a contingency amount of **AT LEAST 15%**. This will cover extras and unavoidable additions which you will usually incur.

To fund the refurbishment and finishing costs, predictions need to be made accurately from the start with regard to conversion costs including fire safety and acoustic insulation, the addition of ensuites and room reconfigurations where necessary. Knowing what you need to do to meet all regulations at the start of the project is vital so that you budget for these seemingly invisible yet fundamental aspects of the build. Draw up a specification that details **WHAT** is needed (this is covered more in the Finish It section) and then you can plan **HOW** to get it and pay for it. Planning the finance at this stage will save you hours of heartache and stress later.

The key calculation you need to assess is how much the property will make in terms of returns, NOT just how much it has cost in the first place. So, for example, if you pay in total

£200,000 for a refurbished 8 – bed HMO and your annual income is £38,000 and your outgoings are £18,000, your annual profit is £20,000.

Easy! In terms of the return on investment the calculation depends on how much money you have left in the property.

So let's say you are able to get a mortgage of £150,000, and therefore you have left £50k in the property.

Your ROI would be (£20,000 (annual profit) / £50,000 (money left in)) x 100 = 40% ROI.

Your yield however is calculated based on the income divided by the overall cost of the development. So to calculate this you need to divide the cost of the development by the annual income you receive.

In this example it would be (£20,000/ £200,000) x100 = 10% yield.

(Please note that this is a simplified version which does not include extra costs you may have incurred such as stamp duty, legal costs etc).

tip22

Ultimately it is the ROI which is the most important figure of which to be mindful. Some people call this ROCE (Return On Capital Employed). If you have created an HMO which is valued at more than you paid for the total development AND you are able to draw out all of your development costs (usually by way of a mortgage) then you can create an infinite return on your investment.

Ideally you will find property deals which allow you to add enough value to take all your money out through re-financing but if you are investing in an area where the yields are high, you might find capital growth is limited. In which case be prepared to leave some money in the development. Over time your investment will grow and enable you to take all your money out, but this might not happen immediately.

tip23

If you are working with another investor or a JV partner it is essential that you plan a regular communication slot for discussion, updates and information exchange. Whether that be a telephone call, Skype call or one-to-one meeting. The relationship you have created and the reputation you build will depend on your ability to be trustworthy and reliable. Even if you have bad news to report, it is far better to do this early on than sit on it and wait, hoping you can correct the issue before your investor discovers anything is wrong. Plan in a regular feedback slot to allow your investor all the information he or she needs. Some investors don't want to know the details of the project as it progresses, others want to know everything step by step. How ever you define your relationship and roles at the beginning, evolution is normal! You may find that your investor becomes a very useful 'critical friend' helping you to solve problems and suggest ideas. Even if you are the project manager, having a person who is an invested 'listening ear' can be a tremendous asset. At the end of the project it is good practice to create a fully detailed spreadsheet statement detailing all the expenditure and income. This then becomes a tool for learning and further application for your next project. It demonstrates your ability to manage costs and budget, and shows the real ROI. It also gives a clear idea of the exit strategy and the true financial picture of the project. Essential if you want to build a portfolio.

tip24

Identify the Key Performance Indicators on your investment early on. What you measure, you treasure! Decide what you want to measure – yield, cash flow, voids, advertising costs, return on investment etc. Even before you have started it is a good idea to think about these areas as they may influence your choice of specification.

tip25

Take **LOTS** of photos and videos of your HMO from the moment you have the keys all the way through until it is ready to let. Don't hold back! They are like forensic evidence for the valuer or surveyor which demonstrate the huge amounts of improvement, value and ultimately positive cash flow your HMO represents. Create a folder where you can keep all the 'before, during and after' photos. The more the merrier! You will need these to create a 'Valuation Pack' when the time comes to have the property valued.

tip26

When you are coming to the final stages of the development, now is the time to create a 'Valuation Pack'. This is a folder that details all the work you have undertaken and is demonstrable evidence of the value you have added to the property. Creating this saves the surveyor or mortgage valuer huge amounts of time of course (not that they'll thank you for it). But it is a great piece of evidence that enables them quickly and proficiently to see you as an investable business, especially in the realm of commercial finance. Your pack should include:

- Before and after photographs
- Plan layout – before and after
- Detailed specification of works
- Schedule of works
- Comparable valuations of properties in area
- HMO Licence
- Buildings certificates (completion statement, and other building regs certificates)
- ASTs (if the property is tenanted before the valuation)

tip27

Work closely with your mortgage advisor at all times. He or she will be in touch with the various lending products available and will be able to assess which one(s) are best for you and your project. Keep in touch with your advisor with friendly notes and reminders, just to keep your case at the forefront of their mind (I think you get my drift).

If you can demonstrate an ability to find, finish, fill and future-proof your HMO investment, you will discover that you become a fascination for financiers! Investors across the world are looking for secure, high yielding investments, and HMOs are no exception. I have completed many deals where money has been left in the deal – but it's not been my money! Giving an investor anything from 7% return upwards is very attractive when banks can only return 1–3% at best. Your track record and ability to systemise and professionalise your business will be the key to creating an investible opportunity. Investors will be fascinated by you, fish for more information from you, and follow you. You therefore need to facilitate a way you can enable a favourable result for you both.

FINISHING IT

The finish of your HMO needs to be decided before you start. As Cicero the famous philosopher said "Before beginning, plan carefully."

You need to be very clear about the type of refurbishment, build or renovation you intend to carry out. Your decisions will emanate from the research you have done into the needs in your local area and lead you to draw certain conclusions. Is there a demand for highly contemporary interiors? Is there a demand good internal storage? Is there a demand for ensuites? Unless you know the demands of tenants and their preferences, AND the cost implications, you will find it hard to decide a strategy to drive forward. It is worth remembering that all types of rooms make it to the market and if priced according to their perceived value, will rent all year round. Rooms with ensuites, mod cons and additional extras will always be perceived to have higher value and thus command a higher price. You may be willing to reduce some of the additional extras in order to get a faster turn-around on the project and to get rental income sooner. One aspect of the build that needs

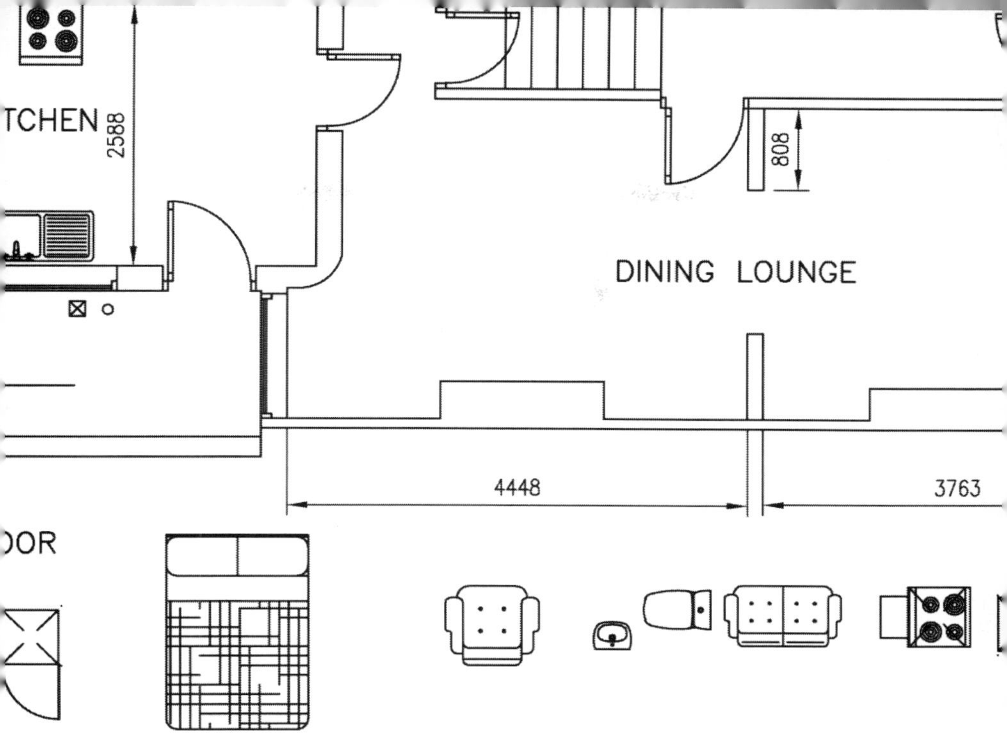

to be budgeted for carefully due to the potential consequences of not getting it right, is fire safety. Correctly fitting fire doors, interlinked smoke detectors, a fire alarm panel, thumb turn locks and sufficient extinguishers need to be planned for within the spec of your project (as a minimum). A useful guide that Local Authorities often refer to is the Homestamp guide (www.homestamp.co.uk) which will detail the minimum fire safety requirements for your particular project. Legislation is always changing and developing in the Private Rented Sector (PRS) so ensure you find a way of learning about new legislation as it is passed (see **Future-Proofing It** for more details). Remember that this book will help you create an HMO for professionals (whether young, middle aged or pre-retirement)! Here, I am specifically addressing this part of the market. In this section, **Finishing It** also refers to **Refurbishing It** and **Furnishing It**.

tip29

While you are still viewing properties and making offers, this is also the time to be identifying potential builders and contractors who you will use to develop the property and turn it into an HMO. In your property POWER TEAM you will need as a minimum:

- Builder
- Plasterer
- Joiner
- Roofer
- Plumber / Gas fitter
- Electrician
- Glazer / Window fitter (preferably FENSA registered)
- Tiler
- Carpet fitter
- Gardener / landscaper
- Painter and decorator
- Possibly an interior designer

Identify builders who have undertaken similar sizes of projects before and their availability. Although your specification might not yet be ready, line up some meetings with a few builders on site ready for your post-completion date so that they see the house as you bought it. At this stage you are ready to drive the plans and specification forward in order to develop an accurate budget and precise timescales. There are various ways to do this including tendering and interviewing. Our favourite and preferred method seems to work well and is as follows:

- Prepare all documentation and plans for the project and property
- Meet builder / contractor at property for walk-through with plans (take 2 copies with you)
- Explain purpose of project, market and aims of property when completed
- Listen to builder's ideas and reflections
- Discuss project specification and plans and take notes on queries and ideas
- If possible show photos of another similar project
- Agree on the scope of works you are asking a quote for
- Understand if there are subcontractors to be used
- Ask for insurance details (good reputable builders will have public liability as standard and if they use subcontractors they should also be registered with CIS)
- Ask to see qualifications and proof of membership or registration with applicable trade bodies
- Ask for at least two people who can give references of other work
- Give builder a copy of the plans with any additional notes made during the meeting
- Agree on a date for a delivery of a quotation

Getting a quote is the first hurdle to overcome when working with a builder and will demonstrate how committed and keen they are to work with you. If they don't hit their own deadline for the quote, this can be an indication of their general attitude to time-keeping! As conveyancing law points out *'Caveat emptor'* (buyer beware)!

bonus tip

Identify the people from your Local Authority and other local services (i.e. Fire Service) who will be able to advise you regarding legislative and safety aspects of HMO development. These include:

a. Housing officer from HMO licensing team
b. Fire Officer
c. Empty homes officer (usually from within Environmental Health) (if relevant)
d. Building control
e. Planning department

It is worth contacting these departments early on and having preliminary discussions with them to understand the local rules and constraints that your property might fall within. Make a list of questions and queries before you pick up the phone or write an email, so that you utilise your time wisely. Use the information you gain from your discussions to feed into the specification of your property.

We split our developments into three phases (which do inevitably run into one another) but allow us to be clear about who is involved and what deliverables are expected.

- **Phase 1** – Prebuild, specification and planning
- **Phase 2** – Refurbishment fitting & kitting
- **Phase 3** – Decorating and interior and exterior finishing

tip 30

STRAIGHT AFTER you have had an offer accepted and have agreed terms with the agent, you must immediately proceed to developing plans for the property. Getting this part of the planning underway BEFORE you finally complete on the sale hugely speeds up the time for the development and allows you to get going almost as soon as you have bought the property. Using an architectural technician or draughtsman will massively help in terms of having professional plans – these will make it much easier to see the opportunities and possibilities provided by a property. The plans will inform the builders and ensure that everyone is working to the same finished product. A good technician will also highlight any issues such as drainage, power supplies, roof angles and use of space. They will see opportunities for adding space, rooms, light and access that might not have occurred to you. Unless you are a technical buildings expert, employing someone to measure and draw accurate plans will save you money in the long term. The plans are also immensely useful to include in your 'Valuation Pack' at the very end of the project.

tip 31

Create a detailed specification which describes all the work you are commissioning, from the width of walls to the detail of the tiles. Along with the visual plans drawn up (the WHAT) your specification provides the detail (the HOW) of the project. Every decision you take before the project starts will reduce confusion and speed up the delivery time. Where will the bed fit in the room? Is there space for 2 bedside tables or just one? Where will the radiator be located? Can extra shelves be built in? In addition, paint colours, carpet styles, furniture and soft furnishings all need to be thought about, planned for and budgeted. The final 'look' and style of your finished HMO depends on it being well-planned and executed from the beginning. Your specification will complement the plans you have had drawn up so that there is written and visual project documentation.

tip32

Utilise the results from your buildings survey to feed into the specification as there may be particular issues that you need to deal with before any other internal or external works can start.

Safety aspects are paramount in an HMO. Consider where gas and electrical meters are sited and whether you need to budget for moving or altering them. If the water flow to the property is not terrific, you may need to upgrade. Understanding all the pre-build specifications will help you manage, plan and budget accurately.

tip33

A few other things to do in practical terms on the day of completion of the sale:

a. Arrange insurance on the property. Understand that the property will be empty for a few months while work is progressing and this needs to be explicitly stated as part of the buildings insurance policy. You will need to shop around for the best rates as they vary hugely across insurance companies.

b. Take meter readings on the day of completion and create new accounts with energy suppliers. It is easy to overlook this when you will have other more exciting work to be getting on with! However, gas and electricity, water and council tax all need to be set up from day one.

c. If you can, say hello to the neighbours and explain what you are doing with the property. You may need to allay their fears! If you can't speak to them personally, pop a handwritten note through the door complete with your contact details. We have found this to be enormously helpful in terms of building good relationships and developing trust. It also helps to smooth out later problems with noise and inconvenience in the midst of building work!

tip34

Get a coded keylock installed somewhere discreet on an outside wall of the property. These can be bought inexpensively on any online retailer, and will save you and your builder HOURS of time running around after keys! The keylock is a small lockable steel casing that can only be opened by way of a code and can be attached safely to a front wall or brick facing. A front door key is safely placed inside and the code is only given to those you approve. So instead of having lots of keys cut and managing them, you just tell the latest workman or contractor what the code is and they can let themselves into the property. Don't remove it when the project is over, as you can then continue to allow maintenance contractors to use it when necessary. The code will need to be changed occasionally to ensure the ongoing security of the property.

tip35

Once you have a quote you are happy with, you need to arrange another more detailed meeting with the builder to agree on the full scope and plans for the project. Discuss who will be paying for what items, as you may be able to achieve better prices than you builder on specific items like kitchens through LNPG (see Tip 36). Agree on timescales and allow the builder to comment on your project plans so that he/she 'buys in' to the project and understands what you are trying to achieve.

tip36

Set up an account with the Landlord's National Property Group. They offer massively discounted products, materials and supplies to member landlords through selected, nationally recognised organisations. (www.lnpg.co.uk).

tip37

VAT. If you are using a builder who is VAT registered, you may be able to pay a reduced rate of 5% VAT on an HMO development instead of the usual 20%. However this depends on the type of conversion you are undertaking and what the use of the property was before it was converted. You will need to have agreement from your builder to charge you at this reduced rate and certain items are not included. This tip alone could save you thousands of pounds! (For further details please see VAT Notice 708: Buildings and construction, HMRC, 2014).

tip38

bonus tip

A great addition to any room is a USB double power socket – tenants can plug 2 normal UK plugs into the main sockets and charge 2 x USB devices on the USB charges. Even updating current sockets to one of these per room is a good idea – see www.screwfix.com.

When creating an HMO from scratch, ensure that each bedroom has adequate heating, lighting and power sockets. We install at least 3 double sockets per room and if light from the window is poor, we will fit an extra light fitting on a wall or ceiling above an area where a desk might be placed.

Energy efficiency. Now that I have mentioned the means of providing energy, I come now to ways to save energy. Many an HMO landlord has been tripped up by extortionate energy costs once the tenants are enjoying the all-inclusive benefits afforded by their hospitable landlord! This tip is within the Finishing It section as it is at this stage when you need to evaluate what energy saving measures you might want to employ. There are a number of ways that you install energy efficient measures including:

a. Solar PV panels. These are mounted on the roof, and capture the energy generated by the sun in the form of light, and convert the light into direct electrical current. Once the direct current has been captured, it runs through a small box called an Inverter, which converts it to the type of electricity used in the house. The panels fit in with the existing home electrical system, and whatever isn't used is then sold back to the National Grid at the set rate called the Feed-in Tariff. Although there is an initial capital outlay to buy the panels and have them fitted, over time it is highly likely that they will repay their initial cost and lower your electricity bills significantly.

b. Loft Insulation. In some areas it is still possible to get free loft insulation either provided by a private company or funded by the local council – check whether your property is suitable (www.energysavingtrust.org.uk).

c. Green Homes Grant. This helps landlords and tenants by allowing them to make energy saving improvements to their rental property without having to pay all the costs up front. Use this service to find out if you can get a grant of up to £10,000 towards the cost of making your home more energy efficient. Improvements you can get a grant for include adding insulation or installing a low carbon heat system. The Green Homes Grant scheme is only available to home owners and residential landlords in England. These improvements can lead to warmer homes and reduced energy bills over time. (For further information contact: www.gov.uk/check-eligible-green-homes-grant).

d. LED / low energy lightbulbs. Although they will cost you more than standard GU10s (or other sizes) it has been claimed that they can reduce your electricity bills by 80%!

sneaky bonus tip

A sneaky bonus tip – when taking photographs or showing rooms you may prefer to have some bright, full energy bulbs fitted – which makes the room bright and appealing. Change them just before the tenant moves in to save on those long-term bills!

tip40

Fully tiling bathrooms saves on long term on maintenance costs, even though they are more expensive to install initially. Walls can be chipped, scratched or marked when they are plastered and just painted and tiles protect against long term damage.

tip41

Take advice and information from your building power team along the way. Unless you have managed a number of building projects already or are a builder yourself, you will discover there are many ways to skin a cat (that's a metaphor for building an HMO). For example, we often find at some point along the way there is a 'shower' conversation. It goes a bit like this:

Builder: "So you want 5 showers in this property, yes?"

Me: "Yes that's right, 5 showers – 4 in the ensuites and 1 in the communal bathroom"

Builder (sharp intake of breath) "I'll have to talk to Pat the Plumber about that"

Me: "That's ok I already have. We agreed that we'll have three electric showers and two off the mains water"

Builder (more sucking of teeth) "And has he said that the water pressure will be enough to deliver that amount of water all in one go? Will the heating be sufficient from the boiler? I'm presuming you'll need to install a pump to deliver that kind of flow?"

Me: "Oh yes, we've already checked the water pressure and it's good and the boiler will be 37Kwh so the flow rate should be sufficient too, and we'll use low-flow shower heads which will help"

Builder: "Hm, well what about a pump? Won't you need that too?"

Me: "Yes we might need one pump as we don't want to install an unvented cylinder in this development"

Builder: "Well I was gonna say about that as it might be better to install an unvented system"

Me: "Well Pat has done a thorough assessment and he is a heating and boiler engineer as well as a plumber you know"

Builder "Hm. Well if you're sure" ... (casts doubtful glance down at specification sheet)". Wanders off muttering to himself "I'd say an unvented cylinder would be the way to go". . .

You will find there are as many views as people on site, so it's important to listen to them all, BUT make a decision based on the one whose experience is most suited to the decision at hand. In this case, I went with Pat the Plumber's advice and all went well. There was enough hot and cold water to each shower, bathroom and tap; water flow was good and even; and no showers have broken down or had to be replaced. Also we managed to keep the costs down by doing it this way.

tip42

Create a project plan from the outset which identifies timescales, decision-points and critical features to keep everyone on track. It should also identify who is responsible for which parts of the delivery of the project. We use standard project management software and spreadsheets as our main tools. These allow us to define actions and show dependencies which helps identify the risks of certain things slipping or other things being delivered faster. You don't have to be a computer whizz kid to write a project plan. You don't even need to know too much about building processes. However to make it work you need to write it in conjunction with your builder and ensure that all works are included and that a timescale is agreed and defined. Using a spreadsheet allows you to list all the jobs and phases of the work on the left, then across the top you plot the time in weeks and days. Define how long each task will take, and who is responsible and on another sheet make a note of the cost estimate. Each week you should be able to identify where the project is on track, where it is slipping and why and what decisions need to be taken to move the project forward.

tip43

Be clear from the start whose role it is to oversee and manage the project and also when and how will they be reporting back (if you are not project managing). We have found that weekly or fortnightly project meetings help to keep things on track and keep the team focused on the next parts of the plan. It also provides a useful check-in to see if anything is drifting and why, and where the budget is being spent. However often it is scheduled it is VITAL that it happens when agreed and on time. Otherwise you will give the impression that it is not important and that you tolerate slippage. YOU know what you want, and that YOU take the lead and make the final decision. If you decide not to project manage the project yourself, find a reliable project manager who you are confident will not only manage the project well but will also reduce your costs along the way.

tip 44

Building projects generally work in four phases – first fix, main build, second fix, decoration. These are all part of the construction phase. Unless you are a builder or tradesperson carrying out the work, the practical delivery of this aspect of development lies squarely with your builder. However, managing the build and ensuring its success lies firmly with you, the client! Hold regular meetings with your lead builder or contractor to assess the pace and development of the project. Whether you are ripping everything off down to the brickwork and starting again from scratch, or just titivating the colour scheme with some paint, regular communication is imperative for the project to come in on time and budget. Managing the cost of your conversion or refurbishment is critical to its overall success. If you don't manage your outlay, your builder will happily do it for you, but he is not paying the price for a badly managed project – you are.

tip 45

Agree stage payments with your builder to ensure the work flows smoothly from one phase to the next. Any hold up in payment may mean he or she moves onto another job. Agree from the outset when and how you will pay, and identify key performance indicators (such as at the end of the first fix, or when the plastering is completed or kitchen fitted) to be achieved before payment occurs. Use your project tools – spreadsheets, plans, GANTT charts to keep track of the work and costs. Your phone will be red hot during this time!

bonus tips

If this is your first HMO conversion, you will be learning much as you go. Write a journal, diary, blog or 'notes to self' so that your learning won't be lost and so that you can improve next time!

"Mistakes are the portals of discovery" said James Joyce. Don't be too hard on yourself when things go wrong. Use mistakes to make discoveries and take as much learning from them as you can. You will never waste the pain of a mistake if you do this.

tip46

You will face a mass of choices along the way in respect of details of kitchen and bathroom fittings, electrical sockets, aerial points, radiators, switches, tiles, windows, doors and other apparently small and insignificant particulars. Some of these cannot be decided before the project gets underway, so you will need to be available to make the decisions in person, or use technology (camera phones, Skype etc) to look at the choices remotely, with your builder in situ. That way he (or she) can visually identify where a socket, light or aerial point could be placed and allow you to decide where it should go.

tip47

Broadband. Like water, tenants expect broadband to be on tap and in full flow 24 hours a day! Sign up for the highest quality broadband service in your area. Even if it's slightly more expensive, having unlimited superfast broadband will not only attract tenants but will help keep them too. Order it early as it can take a few weeks for the delivery of the router, and the line to be activated. Choose a suitable location for a shelf where the router can be placed and kept safe from tampering. Unless there is already a power socket nearby, have one fitted. Once fitted, use a Speedchecker App to test that the download and upload speeds are in accordance with the speeds advertised.

tip48

Consider fitting a masterkey system to your HMO. This is a tiered system of keys that allows the main keyholder's key (the master) to open all doors in a building. The next level of key opens a specific bedroom door and the front and back door and the final level opens just front and rear doors (which is useful for cleaners). Although it is not cheap to install it will literally save HOURS of your time when coupled with a keylock, to enable tradespeople to carry out jobs and maintenance.

---

tip49

Before you furnish the house and add the finishing touches, now is the time to complete a snagging checklist. Go through the house room by room closely examining the quality and execution of the build. Identify any jobs not yet completed or not completed to standard, and create a snagging sheet or list that you can talk through with your builder. For the vast majority of snagged items, your builder should address these without requiring further payment. Hold back some finances as a retainer that is only paid when you are happy that the whole job has been completed. You may have to negotiate on some extra items that crop up but ensure that the builder does not receive the final payment until you have 'signed off' the job in its entirety.

For many weeks you will visit the project and leave with your clothes covered lightly in dust, dirt and grime. Then all of a sudden before you even realise it has happened, the plaster is dry, the tiles are grouted, the kitchen units are installed and the house is ready for decoration. At this point the fun really begins! So as you enter Phase 3 – here are a few hints and tips to help you design the interior so that it lasts long and is hardwearing yet attractive.

tip 50

The number one rule for HMO interior design is to keep it simple! Ideally you will have decided on the colour scheme a long time beforehand, as you will need to tell the decorator the colours for walls and woodwork and any special requirements you have. Remember to consider the long-term implications for your colour scheme. Colours that are fashionable now might not be in a few years' time. In which case have you budgeted for redecorating costs? Minor scuffs and marks will appear after even a couple of months so keep a detailed record of which colours were used first-time round and where, so that paintwork can be touched-up when needed. Although neutral colours may seem bland, remember that you will need to touch-up the paintwork regularly to keep it fresh and clean so having a simple, neutral colour scheme will make it much easier. Matt paint for walls and gloss or sheen-based such as eggshell for woodwork and doors works well. Try and use anti-mould paint in the kitchen and bathroom or anywhere that might be exposed to dampness.

bonus tip

Ensure you buy the paint from the same manufacturer or supplier. Paint shades can differ hugely depending on where you buy it from – one make of magnolia might not match the new make you've bought.

tip51

If you're not sure what colours to accent or highlight in a room, buy curtains first. It's much easier to match wall colours to curtains than the other way round. You can often find cushions and bedding to match curtains thus creating a co-ordinated look for a room which is far more appealing than a mismatched combination of colours. Consider black-out curtain linings or fitting blinds where light might be a problem (such as in a south-facing bedroom).

tip52

Furniture needs to be well-made and robust. Although this goes without saying, many people furnish their HMOs with poor quality furniture and then spend time replacing, renewing or repairing it. For a professional HMO your tenants need hard wearing, quality furniture that will withstand many years of wear. Unless you are experienced in creating an eclectic and unusual interior, it's always best to buy furniture from the same source – at least the basic bedroom items (bed, wardrobe, chest of drawers and bedside table). You are trying to sell quality and not artisan individuality! Make sure you buy them with a warranty and that sofas and mattresses meet flameproof regulations. Often you can get great deals on bedroom packages from companies supplying to the HMO market.

tip 53

Provide enough storage space – we have recently taken to installing built-in furniture to each bedroom as this is far more robust than freestanding furniture, and also enables far greater storage space to be created. If that is not possible, consider under-bed storage boxes, wardrobes with shelves or additional lower drawers, alcoves that could have shelves added, or fitting a small area of kitchen worksurface at waist height in an alcove to create a desk. Generally, as a minimum we provide a double bed with underbed storage and a good quality orthopaedic mattress, a bedside table and light, a chest of drawers, and a wardrobe. Recently we have also been providing flatscreen TVs attached on a bracket to the wall. If you choose to do this, you must consider installing aerial and power sockets during the build phase and CAT6 or CAT5 cabling to enable catch-up TV.

tip 54

Choose floor coverings wisely. We use hardwearing, bleach-cleanable but good quality carpets in all bedrooms, living rooms and on the stairs and landing. We don't use corded, low-grade carpets as this can give a rather cheap impression. Floor tiles are used on the kitchen and bathroom floors and any other areas of high usage such as utility or plant rooms. Whenever we have bought a property that has an original tiled floor in (such as a Minton tiled floor – quite common in Stoke-on-Trent) we have had it cleaned and professionally renewed as it makes a beautiful impression to the entrance of the house. It's also practical too. Avoid laminate flooring in bedrooms and upstairs as it can be noisy and cold. In other types of HMO this flooring works well, but the professional market demands comfort!

tip 55

Ensure you use appliances that are either brand new and in warranty, or if second-hand are PAT tested to ensure they are safe. We discreetly label all shelves in the fridge and freezer with a small sticky number label that corresponds to the room number. We also label all the kitchen cupboard doors on the inside, again with the room number. This clarifies which area of storage is for which tenant and ensures parity from the start!

tip 56

Arrange a thorough clean of the property before you add the finishing touches. We use professional cleaners who clean literally every surface, shelf, tile, carpet, wall and skirting board! They take a whole day to do it but afterwards there is not a particle of dust in existence!

Then the finishing touches can be added such as blinds and curtains, pictures, noticeboards and signage, mirrors, lampshades, and bins. Accessories are a must and are often the things that add character to the house. Incoming post boxes on the hall wall, hooks on the back of doors for coats, and items like drying racks are essential. They also encourage the tenants to put away their things. Mirrors in the hall add light to the area and well-chosen pictures add a homely character to the property. When tenants looks round they will be unconsciously assessing how they feel in the property – therefore warmth, comfort, tidiness and well-ordered space needs to be at the forefront of your thinking when designing the interior. In kitchens we try to use colour-coordinated utensils, tea towels and even kettles and toasters! Ensure you provide enough basic cutlery, crockery, pots and pans and cooking equipment.

bonus tip

Give a flavour of the local area to the house by framing old pictures and maps of the local area (find them on ebay.co.uk) as this generates a great talking point amongst tenants.

tip57

Finally, take a long hard look at the exterior of the property. Does it need a good sweep up outside? How does the front door look? Clean and well maintained or scruffy and dirty? Is there a house number sign to identify this house on the street, or will tenants have to count down til they work out which is your one? The outside 'kerb appeal' will give them the first impression of the property so make sure yours is clean and tidy and has a visible door number!

BROOKLYN

FROM THE STATION

FILLING IT

Just as it is important to create a procedure for Finding, Funding and Finishing your HMO, you also need to have a clear procedure for letting your rooms – Filling It.

In fact this is one of the most important areas to develop as this is the process during which you will really demonstrate how effective you are as an investor. This is when you prove you can create an income stream! If you can't let your rooms, you haven't got an investment. It's as simple as that. You have a liability, not an asset, and it will drain your time, your finances and your emotions. So, focus on Filling those rooms and you will rapidly see an improvement in all three areas. If you are using an agent, you may want to share this section with them!

Now that we have been filling rooms for a few years, we have developed a simple but effective system from start to finish which looks like this:

1. Preparation of room
2. Advertising of room (and house)
3. Phone screening of tenant
4. Viewing
5. Securing room fee
6. Undertaking references
7. Agreeing move-in date
8. Collecting remainder of deposit and rent payment
9. Moving-in and induction
10. Courtesy call

tip58

Before you start advertising or letting any room it is vital that the house and the room are prepared. Ensuring that it is clean and tidy and hoovered is a bare minimum. Not only will this allow you to take better photos for marketing purposes but it allows tenants to imagine what it would be like if they lived there. It is quite possible to show a potential tenant around before everything is completely finished in a newly renovated property. However, you need to know what the finishes, furnishings and contents are going to be so that when asked, you can be clear how the house will be finished. Tenants may ask for details such as what utensils or crockery will be provided? Will there be bike storage? Will you provide chairs and a table outside? Be clear about your answers to these questions even if you haven't yet got around to sorting all those things out. If your house is ready and already has some rooms tenanted, ensure that the room you are advertising is clean, tidy and dressed. If you are advertising a room which already has a tenant, just endure that the tenant is happy for you to carry out viewings giving them 24 hours notice to tidy up. It is always a good idea to arrive early anyway, as their version of tidy might not be yours!

tip59

Dressing a room. As an additional sales tool, the room ideally needs to be dressed. By dressing a room I mean ensuring that it is displayed to its fullest effect so that potential tenants can imagine themselves actually living there, sleeping there and making this their home. This means making the bed with a duvet and cushions, and possibly a throw. Are the pictures straight, the bin empty, the windows clean? Is the living room tidy, cushions plumped and curtains drawn? Turn all the lights on and consider replacing the low energy lights with higher wattage ones for the viewing. Close all the doors and drawers to the furniture. If the room has a slight smell (either from the previous inhabitant or as a result of being new) stick a plug-in air freshener into one of the sockets. Before the viewing you will also need to arrive early to check all the communal areas and tidy up anything which looks obviously off-putting.

Noticeboards. Whether you have a licensed or unlicensed HMO, tenants need to know certain information which will make not only their but also yours (or your agent's) life easier. So as a bare minimum you will need:

a. House Rules
b. Emergency contact details
c. Wifi log in details (and user policy if you have one)
d. Bin collection times (you can download these from your local council's website)
e. Fire exit information

If you have a licensed HMO there are minimum stipulations for noticeboards and signage that are required to be displayed so in addition to these you will need:

a. Your HMO licence. This outlines the number of people the house is licensed for and who is the manager of the property. This is very important as it will determine whether you can take couples or not and also gives the tenants a clear directive about how many people are legally allowed to live in the house. Tenants are pretty savvy about the other residents in the property and notice when the shared bathroom is suddenly being used more often than usual.
b. Gas and fire safety certificates
c. Fire safety and fire escape notices. In addition to a fire escape notice on the general noticeboard, all bedrooms need to have a fire escape notice locally. Depending on the complexity of the fire escape route, you may also want to put up fire escape stickers that clearly show the escape route

bonus tip

As well as noticeboard information, create a folder in the kitchen for all the appliance guides, and useful information such as bus timetables and a map of the local area. This folder can also include safety test schedules such as emergency lighting discharge and fire alarm testing. That way, you always have a local record of when the tests were carried out.

tip61

Tenants find information crib sheets useful when using appliances such as the oven, microwave, washing machine dishwasher and tumble dryer. If you are going to create these, ensure they are laminated and posted near the appliance. Items such as fridge freezers, the iron, and kettle are usually self-explanatory!

Advertising the room

tip62

Setting the rent. Before you can advertise the rooms, you need to ascertain from your local knowledge what the current and expected level of room rent is in your area. This information will have formed part of your original due diligence, so it is likely that you are already familiar and confident about what you can achieve. Remember that certain aspects of rooms achieve higher rents, such as ensuite rooms. It is a fine art setting room rents as it not only depends on local competition for rooms, but also times of the year (we have found winter rent levels to be lower), whether local businesses are recruiting, and what local house prices are doing. Also if you are re-letting a room and demand has changed in your area, you may need to re-consider the rent you are asking. Raising (or lowering it) it by a few pounds per week will not make too much impact on the tenant, but will allow you to increase your profits by reducing voids and increasing income. You will need to be assiduous about keeping abreast with local prices in order to ensure that your rates are correct for your local market. Remember that VOIDS are a LOSS in income to you. Here's a mathematical problem for you: How long will it take to recoup the loss on a room that is priced at £100 per week if it is empty for a fortnight? Ok, so it was a trick question. You can't recoup the loss, unless you raise the rent by a considerable figure per week. The loss is a loss. However, the loss you have made is £200. Some landlords refuse to reduce their rent because they believe their room is 'worth every penny of £100 per week'. Well in a buoyant market that might be true. But if there are a glut of rooms and yours has stood empty for a few weeks you may want to re-think your strategy. Although I don't believe in heading for the lowest common denominator, price is still a sensitive gateway for many HMO tenants. So consider whether it would be worth reducing the rent by £10 per week to see what response you get. After all a full room is an income-producing asset. An empty one is a **LIABILITY**.

---

tip63

Take high resolution, good quality photographs of the property before it is tenanted or when it's in its most favourable condition. This will save you hours of time and effort later. Use a good camera (not a phone camera) to get wide angle shots and if necessary pay a professional. If you are taking on an HMO which is already up and running, then you need to choose a good time to prepare the house and rooms without disturbing the current tenants too much. If the house is empty after Finishing It, this is an excellent opportunity to spend a whole day taking the photos which will last you many years to come. Ensure each of the rooms is dressed and use your critical eye to identify any features, quirks or areas you either do or don't want to focus on. This might be the only opportunity you have to take marketing photos while the house is looking its best. Don't waste it!

bonus tip

Shoot a short video of the property with your voice-over describing the house and its features. No need to go into details about room rates as these might change. Simply walk through the house and describe it in a friendly way as if you were guiding someone on a personalised viewing. You can later upload this to various websites or social media sites as an additional advertising tool.

tip64

Create your advert. Use the acronym AIDA to formulate your advert –

- Attention
- Interest
- Desire
- Action

Give your advert a catchy title – 'Spacious double ensuite with comfy bed' will generate more interest than 'Large double bedroom available'. Use adjectives that make your room stand out in the title by highlighting its features and don't make the title too long. You are trying to grab the reader's attention in your title to pique their interest and persuade them to read further. Describe the house and room(s) as fully as possible but remember to list the benefits as well as the features. So rather than saying 'Near to shops and supermarket' say 'Near to shops and supermarket – only 5 minutes walk away, a real time saver'. You will generate desire by using descriptions that create a desirable emotional response, so use words such as 'warm, spacious, light, airy, clean, beautiful, gorgeous, comfortable'. As well as writing a factual advert, your advert also must persuade the reader that this house will meet all their needs and provide them with a fantastic experience of shared living. Finally add a call to action: 'Book your viewing now before all these rooms are gone!', 'Only 1 room left – call today to book a viewing'. Creating a sense of urgency and scarcity propels the reader to pick up the phone or text you to arrange a viewing.

Research shows that adding good quality, high resolution photos of your property generates more replies to adverts which in turn leads to greater number of viewings which in turn increases rent! So ensure that you also upload or include photographs in your advert. These should show:

- Communal room (such as kitchen or living room)
- Bedroom
- Close-Up bedroom feature (such as picture, light, window)
- Bathroom (or ensuite)
- Front of house / or other bedroom or communal view

If you are advertising more than one bedroom, use the photo of the best room and add a tagline that states 'Lovely bedroom interior – typical of this house'. Putting the communal room photo first sets the scene for the backdrop of the rest of the property and acts as a kind of entrance into the house. Adding a photo of a close-up bedroom feature allows the advert to stick in people's minds and generates a good talking point later too. If the front view of the house is not particularly appealing, add another bedroom or communal area photo. If you haven't got enough photos of the house – try to get some next time you are there, or alternatively use a 'lifestyle' shot such as a group of young professionals laughing together, or a soft-focus picture of a nice meal. This subliminally creates a sense of attraction to your property.

tip65

Although there are specialised websites (www.spareroom.com and www.easyroommate.co.uk) for room rentals, consider others such as Open Rent which is a cheaper option but also advertises on Right Move. Ensure you have your own website too where you can advertise available rooms and also give prospective tenants an idea of what they can expect from your property.

tip66

Don't just rely on one website for advertising your rooms. There are a growing number of other portals and social media sites where 'word-of -mouth' shares can rapidly expose your advert to a much wider number of people and generate interest much more quickly. A catchy paragraph and a couple of good quality photos can spread like wildfire on Facebook! Even non-digital forms (such as newspapers, leaflets and signage) are effective forms of advertising. However, ensure you target your audience rather than use a scattergun approach which will waste your time and money. Focus on a couple of local large employers, building a relationship whereby you can take in leaflets and information about the rooms. If necessary offer to incentivise them for any leads which result in a room booking.

tip67

Once you start the process of advertising collect every email, phone number and name of each person who inquires about the property. This can become a very useful contact list a few months down the line when you have another vacancy to fill! (A great email client is www.mailchimp.com which allows you to create templates and re-use them with updated details whenever you have a vacant room. Prospective tenants can unsubscribe from the list if they no longer wish to receive the emails).

tip68

In order to rent a room quickly you have to reply to requests for viewings fast and promptly. In a growing and competitive market, the initial impression you give is vital. As soon as you have interest from a prospective tenant, call them to arrange a time to view. Take their name, mobile phone number and email if possible. On this call ascertain the timeframe for their move, their budget and their occupation. A lot of time can be wasted on viewings where the tenant is speculatively looking, or their contract is not confirmed or they have misread the rental amount. This also gives you an opportunity to build rapport and create a professional impression.

---

tip69

If you have a lot of interest, you may find block bookings work best in terms of your time. Most tenants will want to view at evenings or weekends. It may take some to-ing and fro-ing to arrange a suitable time, so bear this in mind! Once you have a time and date agreed, note this in your diary and include the telephone number of the person. Always confirm the viewing with a text message to the prospective tenant with the address of the property including postcode and this message:

- "Dear xxx, I am looking forward to meeting you at xxxx [address] tomorrow night at 6.30pm. If you have any problems, please feel free to call or text. Many thanks Wendy"

Then 45 minutes or so before the viewing, send a reminder text:

- "Dear xxx, I am texting to confirm the viewing at xxxx [address] at 6.30pm tonight. See you soon"

tip 70

Arrive early and make sure the house is ready for the viewing (as outlined above). During the viewing, make sure you are friendly and open – ask questions of the tenant as well as showing them round. You may need to undertake some sales training if you are not used to selling, as not only do you need to 'sell' the house and the rooms to the prospective tenant, you need to be able to listen to their needs and match the offering to what they want. It is really important at this stage to create a conversation rather than an inquisition and as you listen to their answers, you can use these to 'help' the PT (Prospective Tenant) choose your room over others they might see. You will want to find out

- When are you looking to move? [Between a fortnight and a month is the best length of time – if it is longer or shorter than that you need to consider a) why the tenant needs to move so soon, or b) can you hold the room that long?]
- Where will you be working? (What is the job role, salary, contract length etc)
- Where are you currently living? (if they are living locally already you may want to know the reason for the move)
- If I ask for a reference from a past landlord will I get a good report? (A very telling question)!
- Do you have any CCJs or outstanding debts that I need to know about? (A key question that enables you to identify their honesty as you will discover the truth when you reference them)
- Do you smoke? (not necessarily a deal-breaker, but nevertheless useful to know)
- What are you ideally looking for in a property? (A great opportunity to match the features of your property with their preferences)
- Have you got a girlfriend/ boyfriend/ partner? (Useful to know in case of long-term sharing risks)
- My rooms rent really quickly and I already have another couple of people who are really keen to view soon, so why should I choose you over them? (A direct question which will give you a real insight into the real person)!

Finally use your gut instinct. If you don't think this person is right for the room or the property, it's always better to be honest. If you need some time to think about it, make an excuse like 'I have another couple of viewings later and I really promised to show the other people round, so I'll call you later to discuss the room if that's ok?' Then call them and be frank and let them know you don't think they are right for the house and the reason why.

---

tip 71

Understand what the process if for letting a room. Can you communicate it in three sentences or less? If you can't, you need to practice it until it becomes an automatic part of your process. Tenants will have more confidence in you if they feel you understand and are confident with the process. You will also need to have the full suite of forms for renting a room and understand the process for letting a room to a tenant. We find that if the house is fully prepared, and the tenant has responded appropriately to the advert, and this process is done correctly, 9 out of 10 times they take the room.

bonus tip

If the tenant tries to negotiate the rent, be open to this but use this opportunity to trade something in your favour. So if they ask for a £20 reduction, you could suggest that they move in by the end of the week. Or you could ask whether they would consider taking on some part of the responsibility of the property (such as the Responsible Lead Tenant role – see Future-Proofing It).

tip 72

If the tenant decides to take the room you need to take some form of payment to secure the room and remove it from any further advertising. At this point, the prospective tenant should complete an initial application form (see ideas below about how to reduce the paper trail) which outlines their basic information and gives you enough information to gather references. The information gathered needs to include personal details such as name, current address, telephone number and email; their job and salary details; the details of referees and in what capacity are they known by the referee; and information about identification being provided. Then they need to sign the form and agree to continuing with the process for becoming a tenant (i.e. having a credit check undertaken). It is illegal to charge admin fees for setting up a tenancy, but you can ask for a down-payment to reserve the room which is deducted from the overall deposit when the tenant moves in. We also try to ensure that the deadline for moving in is agreed at the same time as the reservation down-payment is made.

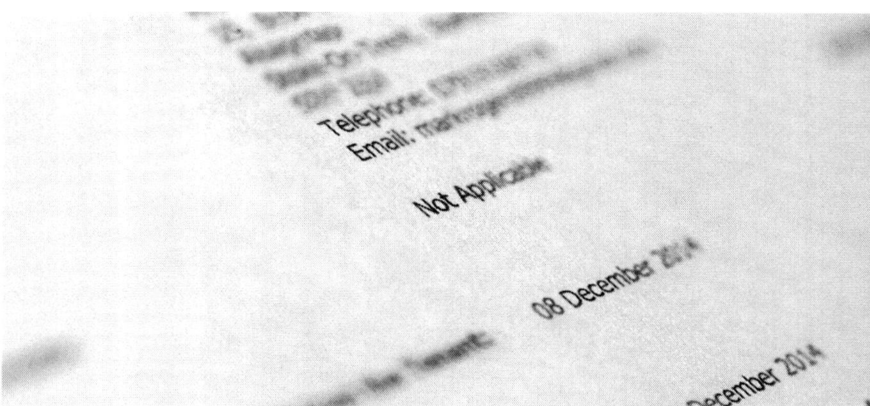

tip 73

As soon as you get into the realm of PAPERWORK and PAYMENTS you need to seriously think about how to work smartly and how to reduce the friction on the transaction. This is one of the most time-and-resource consuming aspects of managing a professional HMO if you aren't careful. Without good systems you will be printing, filing and posting paper all day long!

- Document creation & sharing – use Google Docs, or Dropbox to upload forms (use Google Forms for automatic online form creation) and files to the web where they are automatically backed-up and stored safely.
- Document signing – use www.docusign.com or www.signnow.com which will allow you and your tenant to sign documents electronically and share them once signed
- Deposit or initial fee payment – set up Paypal or Pingit and download your bank's app to your phone so that you can ask your tenant to pay immediately with online banking and transfer the money direct to you whilst at the property!
- Referencing – we use www.lettingref.co.uk where tenants complete the details themselves (including a guarantor's details when necessary) and then you receive an email notifying you when the information has been collected. There are many online systems available but we have found this to be the easiest, most cost-effective and detailed one for us.

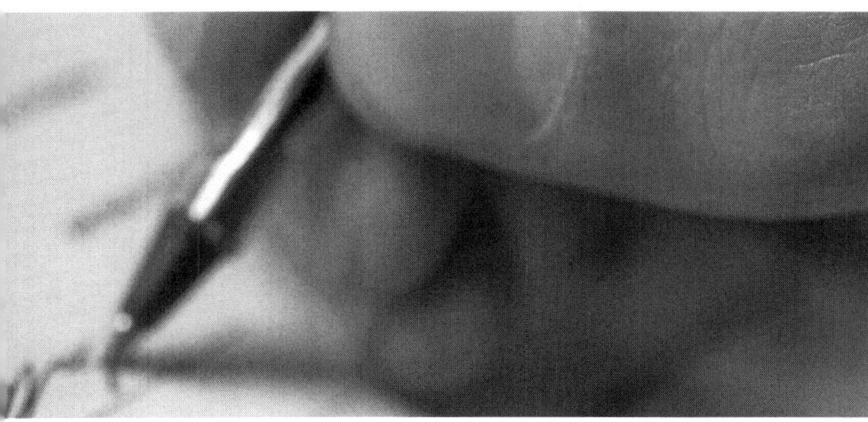

tip 74

A perfect tenant is courteous, flexible, smart, non-smoking, accommodating, reliable, honest, always pays the rent on time and never bothers the landlord over trivialities, never complains or has noisy parties, never annoys the neighbours or other tenants. Can you let me know if you get a tenant like this please as I can offer them a very nice HMO to live in! Very occasionally you may get a tenant like this, but to be on the safe side you need to reference. Remember if you have doubts about the credit worthiness of a tenant, you do not have to accept them as a tenant in the property. However, assuming they have passed the initial stages and you are happy for them to rent a room it is vital to carry out references. There are five steps you can take to check out a prospective tenant. The first three are essential and the other two are optional depending on your time and resources.

1. Credit reference

You can use an online system (as described above) to do this and it will cost between £15 – 45. However this gives you a very useful starting point and if you're not happy about the report or results that come back you may decide to ask for a larger deposit from the tenant or indeed ask them for a guarantor. I think this is a vital aspect of the referencing process as it allows you to see if the potential tenant'(s) has/have any CCJs or other formal financial claims against them which they should have already disclosed.

2. ID checks.

You should verify that your prospective tenant is who they say they are. Potential tenant'(s) need to show you some identification (ID) with a photo such as a passport or European style driving licence along with another form of ID such as a utility bill.

3. Bank statements

Ideally your potential tenant'(s) income should be two and a half times the rent – so if the rent is £100 per week, your tenant should be earning £250 per week. Simples! To demonstrate this you will need to see the last 3 months bank statements, which also provide an invaluable insight into the financial position of your prospective tenant. Is the tenant paid what they say they are? What are the tenants' regular out-goings? Do they regularly get overdrawn? If the prospective tenant refuses, they may have something to hide, in which case you have a right to be wary. Most good tenants won't even question it.

4. Employers reference
This should simply confirm the employment status of the tenant. Is the tenant employed where they say they are? Importantly is the prospective tenant on a full time contract or is their temporary contract just about to finish? It should also give you their salary details which is useful in assessing the tenant's ability to pay.

5. Personal / Business references
When an applicant is currently living in rented accommodation it is useful to obtain a reference from their existing landlord. I would suggest asking the landlord:

- How long has the applicant for the tenancy been a tenant of the current landlord?
- What is / was the rent paid to the current landlord?
- Was the rent paid in full and on time each month to the current landlord?
- Were there any periods where the rent was in arrears?
- Is the rent currently in arrears with the current landlord?
- Has the applicant for the tenancy cared properly for the investment property and its' contents?
- Would the current landlord accept the applicant for the tenancy as a tenant again?

It is always better to call and speak in person to a previous landlord as it is quite possible for tenants to create a previous landlord's reference.

You may want to discuss your findings with them and ask for more detailed information. You may also wish to ask for the details of a guarantor to guarantee their rent should anything go awry. Once you have carried out the referencing report, download the files and keep them in the tenant's folder that you have created. Tell them that the referencing process has been successful and make arrangements for them to move in.

tip 75

Once you have an agreed moving in date, you need to write (well email) the new tenant and confirm all the information about the tenancy including the length of tenancy agreed, the payment period, the rental amount, the deposit and the bills. At this point confirm that the balance of the deposit and the first month's rent (or week's depending on how often they are paying) needs to be in your bank account 24 hours before they move in. You may also wish to email the Assured Shorthold Tenancy document to allow them to read it through before signing it. Using an online signatory system means we don't have to rely on paper-based documents which hugely helps in terms of time, expense and keeping an audit trail!

Starting off with the tenant paying their rent electronically directly into your account usually means that their direct transfer or standing order will continue that way. DON'T accept cash payments as this will only ever create problems and may cause the tenant never to set up an automatic standing order.

tip 76

Before the tenant moves into the property you need to prepare the following items:

- The Assured Shorthold Tenancy (unless done electronically)
- An inventory
- A property Welcome Pack
- The key (plus copies of other keys if necessary)
- The Move-In Checklist

tip 77

When the tenant arrives to move-in, welcome them! Prepare a tenant 'Welcome Pack' that provides the tenant with everything they need to know about their tenancy whilst in your property. This is in addition to the legal Assured Shorthold Tenancy agreement which is the legal contract that binds them and you to the tenancy. The Welcome Pack includes details such as

- Who to contact in an emergency
- Useful utility numbers
- Useful local numbers
- Wifi & broadband information
- Masterkey system (if you have this) and cost of replacing their key
- Security
- Repairs
- Bins
- House Rules
- Form to sign and accept the rules
- (This needs to be talked through with the tenant on induction)

Set expectations from the start particularly with regard to communication. When tenants move in, explain what they should do in the event of

- An emergency
- A repair
- Any queries or concerns they want to report

As well as including this information in a 'Welcome Pack' or 'Induction Manual' keep this information visible on a noticeboard or folder in the communal area.

Then you will need to find a place in the kitchen to go through all the paperwork and details that they need to know. Talk them through the AST and explain their legal obligations and duties, and also what you will do as their landlord. This then needs two signatures on the back of both copies. If this is being done electronically, it can be signed before the tenant moves in.

tip 78

Identify the kitchen cupboard they will use, and the fridge and freezer space for them. Explain the masterkey system and the importance of keeping the key safe. Take the details of their key number. Also remind them of the house rules which they must abide by (as should any of their guests). Ensure you give another tour of their room – demonstrating small things like how to lock the window, how to keep their personal belongings safe, and how to use any equipment such as TVs. In the bathroom (or ensuite) show them how to turn on and off the shower and the extractor fan. Basic though it seems, we have had phonecalls from tenants who were not familiar with UK hardware and wanted to know how to put the door on the snib! Finally make sure you offer them a warm welcome and give them some time to think of any questions that they may have. Assure them of your availability and the process to follow if they have a query, question or concern.

tip 79

If you have the opportunity to introduce the new tenant to any of the existing tenants either before or as they move in, so much the better. Nothing performs as good a welcome as a current tenant. However, in the event that your new tenant hasn't yet come across someone already living there, it's a good idea to drop all the current tenants a line to say that they have a new sharer, whose name is x and they are in room y and could they pop by to say hi next time they are around. This breaks the ice and lets everyone become acquainted.

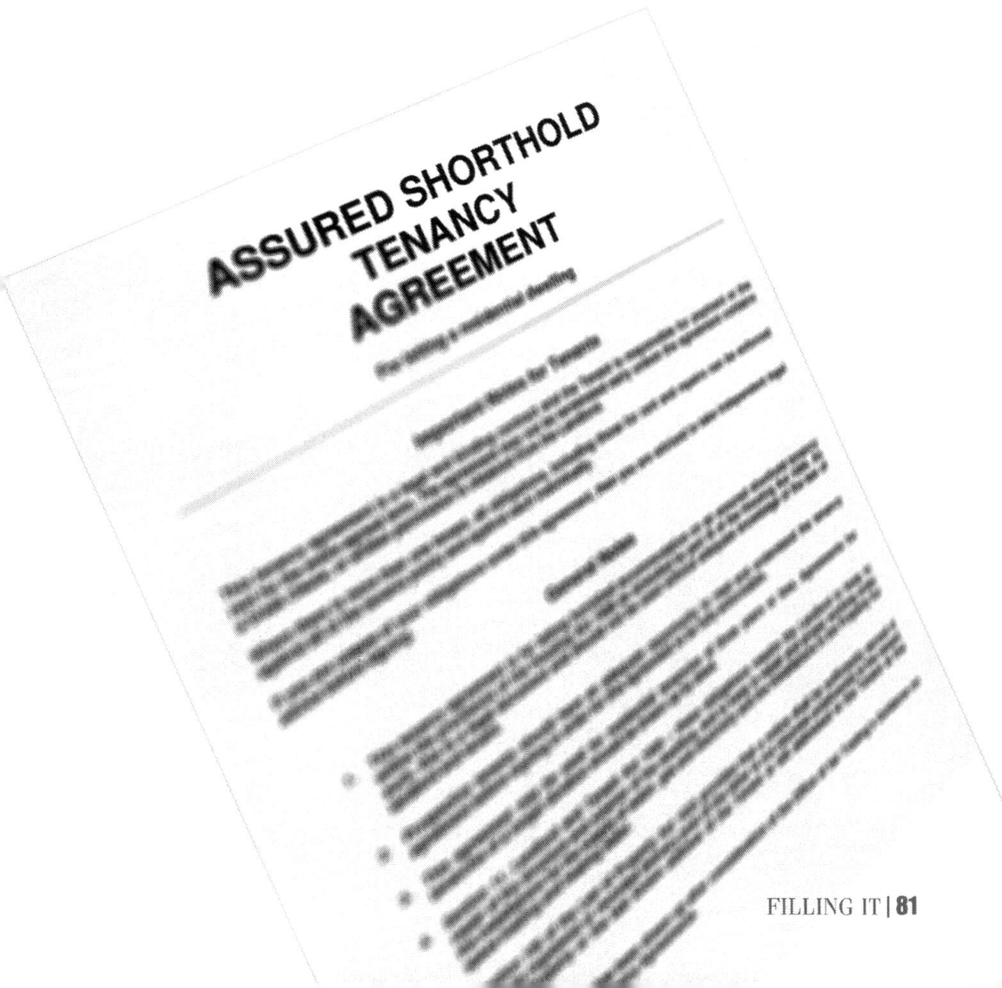

tip 80

A week after your new tenant has moved in call them, email them or text them to ask how everything has gone and check that they are settling in well. Any problems can be ironed out faster and any teething problems dealt with. You can reiterate your commitment to the standards they can expect (and outline your office hours too)!

At this point, you need to ensure that all the paperwork (electronic or real) is filed and indexed. You need to bond the deposit either using the custodial or insured scheme (for more details go to the Deposit Protection Service www.depositprotection.com). Then serve the Prescribed Information from the DPS which can be done direct to their inbox from the DPS if they have paid direct (which they can do via Paypal).

FUTURE-PROOFING IT

It would be easy to sit back and relax after all that hard work refurbishing, finishing and filling your HMO.

Indeed having a celebration after all that hard work would be perfectly commendable! But the hard work is not over yet. Unless you Future-Proof your investment you will soon find that your HMO will be bringing you smaller and smaller returns and more and more problems. So this section focuses on the final part of the puzzle – how to create systems and processes that allow you to maximise your profits and minimize your costs while still providing excellent service and value to your customers – your tenants. The most effective way to future-proof your HMO is in the form of systems. Many people say it but few do it as it is dull, time consuming and requires great attention to detail. However, once set in motion, your systems will allow you more free time, more profit, fewer problems and more enjoyment of your HMO. Yes I said it – enjoyment!

Once your HMO is systemised you can much more easily bring other people into the business with a clearly defined role, as they implement the systems you have created. If you are using an agent who has their own systems, this section provides a quality assurance checklist against which you can measure the performance of your agent and even help him or her improve their business. If you choose to use a rental agent, you may wish to use these hints and tips to assure yourself of the quality of management you are getting. Many lettings agents don't have HMO experience or if they do are prepared to let problems slip and slide for weeks. If your agent is not as committed as you are to future-proofing your investment, you may need to look elsewhere or hire your own staff to work to your standards. [Or alternatively buy your agent a copy of this book!]

This section is divided into the three main parts of this process which are:

- Maintaining Customers
- Management of the HMO
- Maintenance of the HMO

tip81

You are renting to a sector of the market place who may themselves be working in a sales-driven, customer focused environment. If you don't provide great customer service and value for money, your customers will look elsewhere. I use the term 'customer' deliberately, because your tenants ARE your customers. They buy from you for at least 6 months (if not 9 months or more), and each month they pay you for the room and house. It is therefore your responsibility as the landlord or investor to ensure that they get the very best service they can from you. By future-proofing our HMOs and keeping tenants happy, our average length of let is 22 months and our occupancy rates are 94%. (Calculated by how many days per annum a room is vacant). Retaining customers takes time and effort but you'll find that as you do this you will remain optimally attractive to new tenants too. When rooms become vacant it will be easier to advertise them well, and fill them too because you will have remained on top of your business and not let it get on top of you!

bonus tip

Treasure what you measure! I've said it before and I'll say it again – if you want to understand your business and what works and what doesn't work, measuring certain key indicators is vital. Only then will you be able to see whether you have one particular room that rents well, or doesn't rent well; whether there is a pattern to the complaints you get at one HMO from another; or whether there is a type of tenant who creates more problems than another.

tip82

Communicating with tenants regularly takes time and effort but can rapidly reduce the amount of hassle and time that is spent managing the property AND increase the length of their tenancy. Simple steps like a monthly group email lets your tenants know that you care about the quality of their experience in the property. It's a great, easy-to-use automatic email system that allows you to schedule emails in advance. So you can cover topics like 'Health and Safety' or 'Clean and Tidy' or 'Friends Staying Over?'. You can gently cover topics that might become issues or risks to the overall smooth-running of the house by introducing the topic and then saying something about it in the main body of the email. We have found this reduces rather than raises queries, as tenants then understand procedures and policies more clearly and also what kind of behaviour is expected of them!

---

tip83

A tenant may choose to move out due to changes in work, or for personal reasons. Ideally you will receive at least a month's notice (stipulate this in your contract). Ensure you have as robust a check-out process as your check-in process, so that the leaving goes smoothly and the room is then ready for the next tenant. On the agreed date that the tenant is moving out, you need to meet the tenant at the property and check the room and inventory. Ensure you check ALL areas such as the kitchen and utility/ laundry areas and any outside shared areas.

Check that all personal items have been removed and that the room is clean and well-presented. Make sure all food has been removed from the cupboards and fridge freezer. Ideally, everything should be ready for a new tenant to move straight in. However, this must be stated to the tenant in the check-out process when they give notice to quit.

tip84

If all has gone well, the rent is up to date and the room is left clean and tidy, then you can return the deposit to the tenant. However, if there are arrears on the account you will need to ask them to pay the arrears before they can receive their deposit back. The best way to avoid this is of course to manage arrears as soon as they arise! Don't let tenants fall behind with their rent without addressing the problem, and if that means taking legal action then you will need to do just that.

tip85

If you find that there is no other way to deal with a non-paying, antisocial or otherwise problematic tenant then you will need to evict them. I have found that HMO tenants are much easier to evict than those in single-let houses. Probably because they are aware of the shared nature of their housing. You must follow the correct procedures for eviction and a couple of useful websites are www.landlordlaw.co.uk and www.landlordzone.co.uk/documents which have plenty of information about how to evict tenants. The most crucial piece of advice I can give when dealing with difficult or problematic tenants is to nip it in the bud. Don't let the problem wear you or the other tenants down. Be professional and calm, and remember the size of the problem is limited to the size of your experience. If you have never experienced this problem before, it will seem huge but if you ever have to address this issue again, you will already be more experienced and knowledgeable and therefore, confident.

tip86

Advertise a room as soon as it becomes vacant ensuring the photos and information is up to date and highlighting any upgrades or new features that might be attractive. Although your old advert might be perfectly serviceable, it is always a good idea to refresh and re-visit it to make improvements. Use your contacts database to advertise the room and email those people who initially showed interest a few months previously. You never know whether their situation has changed and they now need to move. Your room might be just what they need now!

---

tip87

Incentivise your tenants to stay loyal. What could you do to thank someone who has rented from you for over a year? Been a reliable tenant? Helped out when things have gone wrong? What about a bottle of wine or an Amazon voucher? It doesn't need to be much but it just says that you appreciate their custom!

tip88

Bins! I have never been in an HMO where there is not some kind of problem with 'bin' management. Much like small children, bins seem to resist any effort to bring them under control, preferring to take over an otherwise organised and peaceful environment with smells and mess! Whether they are overflowing in the kitchen; contain the wrong type of rubbish; or tenants are confused about when they are collected – BIN policies are part of running a successful HMO. Signage that shows bin collection times are VITAL on your most obvious noticeboard – usually the one in the kitchen.

tip89

Try to find a tenant who will take responsibility for 'low-level' aspects of house management such as waste organisation, bulb replacement and communicating of problems that other tenants haven't raised. In our HMOs we call this role (very grandly) the 'Lead Responsible Tenant' role. The first characteristic of this person is that they have to be willing to take on the role. It will not work if you try to press-gang someone into taking on the role. I tend to identify quite early on which of the tenants seems to be the one who communicates most about issues in the house, and NOT just the one who does the most complaining! The role is a paid position (the princely sum of £15 per month) and we have a role description outlining the duties of this person. I have found this works really well in ensuring that there are sufficient bin bags, washing up liquid and other cleaning consumables, that the bins get put on the street and collected once empty. It means that all the other tenants live in a much more organised environment and the lead tenant is happy too! If you can't find someone who will agree to the role, you will have to find a way to ensure the bins are emptied regularly. Otherwise they smell, become a health hazard and become a brilliant magnet for creating anti-social feeling amongst other local residents.

tip 90

Tenant communication systems. Whoever is in charge of the management of your HMO will be responsible for liaising with tenants, answering their queries and questions and dealing with complaints and problems. Unless you have a great system, you will find that this aspect of managing can be overwhelming especially if you encounter an emergency and find that you have to deal with 9 angry tenants throughout the day! Using a telephone answering service is invaluable as it allows all calls to be answered and dealt with professionally while freeing up your time to attend to other aspects of the business. I have found that tenants like having ONE number to call and don't cope well if you give them a variety of different numbers to call depending on the severity of the issue. Therefore in Best Nest our system is simple – in office hours the phone is available and answered within couple of rings. In out of office hours the phone is diverted to an answering service which takes a message and immediately sends a text and email to two named staff members. We have a rota as to who is in 'emergency stand-by' cover at evenings and weekends. This person then deals with the emergency knowing the processes to follow already. The following day (or when the office re-opens) the emergency is followed up and noted in our 'Emergency situations' tracker spreadsheet. This details the occurrence, the action taken by whom, and the follow-up required.

tip 91

Keys can become a major headache for a landlord (or agent) if you don't have a clear system for managing and tracking them. If you don't want to go to the expense of installing a masterkey system (although I would heartily recommend it particularly if you wish to scale up your business), you need to develop a system using a spreadsheet and large cabinet! Code each keyring so that you know which door the key opens in each property, always have at least one copy made and track them as they leave and enter your office!

tip92

Whether you have a licensed or unlicensed HMO it is imperative that you create systems for managing all the health and safety aspects such as fire alarm testing, emergency lighting testing and discharge schedule, gas and electrical safety checks and PAT testing of appliances. Under The Housing Act 2004 and The Management of Houses in Multiple Occupation (England) Regulations 2006 there are more requirements listed in legislation for those with HMOs over five rooms, whether or not they are licensed. These include the requirements

- to provide essential contact information to each occupier
- to take safety measures (such as fire precaution, escape routes etc)
- to maintain water supply and drainage
- to supply and maintain gas and electricity
- to maintain common parts, fixtures, fittings and appliances including any garden which should be kept in a safe and tidy condition
- to ensure that each unit of living accommodation within the HMO and any furniture supplied with it are in clean condition at the beginning of a person's occupation of it and that every window and other means of ventilation are kept in good repair
- to provide waste disposal facilities

For more information see
www.legislation.gov.uk/uksi/2006/372/pdfs/uksi_20060372_en.pdf

My Five Management Essentials for creating a scalable, leveraged and highly efficient HMO business

1. Masterkey system & keylock on each property
2. Remote answering service which directs all calls appropriately
3. Tenant manager (responsible for advertising rooms, and viewings and then overall management of tenants)
4. Cleaner / Maintenance person (who also checks fire safety equipment and does a bit of garden tidying and who does proactive and reactive maintenance)
5. Lead responsible tenant in each property

What will you need to do then?

- Possibly some finances and rent checking (although your tenant manager could do this).
- Analysing the flow and efficiency of your business
- Identifying improvements and investments
- Overseeing & managing your staff

Systemising your business by documenting each process on one-side of an A4 sheet of paper. Keep it short, keep it implementable! All of which could take less than 5 hours a week for a portfolio of up to 50 rooms. There are some great apps and tools on the internet that can massively reduce your time in running your business (such as Evernote, Hive, Property Hawk, www.10ninety.co.uk). Use them to help you run efficiently, smartly and smoothly, and teach your team to do the same. After that, you may have to consider book-keeping help and employing more staff.

tip93

bonus tip

A great way to send group texts is with www.mightytext.com which allows you to type texts from your computer and send a message to a number of people at once.

One of the key reasons why tenants move house is because of maintenance work that fails to get attended to. Every quarter, your manager/agent/ yourself should diarise a thorough maintenance check of all aspects of the HMO. This needs to be a detailed list that includes all aspects of the fabric and fixtures and fittings of the property, from guttering to glassware, from tiles to taps. You need to assess each element carefully and make a note if it needs cleaning or upgrading, repairing or replacing. Carrying this out each quarter (spring, summer, autumn & winter) will allow you to identify problems before they arise and take action to address them. It will also give you useful data that will enable you to predict likely problems, and use that knowledge for other projects or future HMOs. The information you gather from the maintenance check can be communicated to the tenants too, in the form of feedback – so try to find some areas where you can give positive praise after the maintenance check as well as room for improvement! And don't forget to inform all tenants that someone is coming at least 24 hours in advance. Logging emergencies and other issues that crop up, over time you will gather a much more detailed understanding of how to solve problems and prevent them from occurring in the first place.

tip94

Compile and re-compile a list of tradesmen and maintenance people who you can work with to undertake the routine and emergency work that will no doubt be required from time to time, no matter how well you have Finished It! Always have a preferred supplier and a back-up for the times when your original tradesperson isn't available. You may wish to set up a retainer or a regular payment to maintain the flow of availability. There are companies that offer landlord emergency cover for a small monthly charge and ensure an immediate emergency response to any problems in the property.

---

tip95

Remember the keylock that you installed earlier when Finishing It? Well this is when it really comes into its own! Whenever you have a tradesman that needs access to the house (either routinely, for upgrades or for emergencies) the last thing you want to do is to have to meet them there! Simply tell them the code for the house, where the keylock is located, and hey presto, they can gain access to the house with the key inside the keylock without the need for your presence. Ensure you change the code regularly to maintain validity of your insurance.

---

tip96

You **MUST** stay up to date with legislation relating to property and housing. Recent legislation that has been passed and which relates to landlords, letting agents or HMOs includes:

- The Alternative Dispute Resolution for Consumer Disputes (Competent Authorities and Information) Regulations 2015
- The Consumer Rights Act 2015

- The Deposit Protection Service (DPS) has published new scheme terms and conditions for its custodial scheme
- The Heat Network (Metering and Billing) (Amendment) Regulations 2015)
- The Energy Efficiency (Private Rented Property) (England and Wales) Regulations 2015
- The Smoke and Carbon Monoxide Alarm (England) Regulations 2015
- The Health and Safety Executive's "Legionnaires' disease: the control of legionella bacteria in water systems revised version of their Approved Code of Practice
- The Licensing of Houses in Multiple Occupation (Mandatory Conditions of Licences) (England) Regulations 2018

Whilst ignorance might be bliss, it won't pay your court fees and compensation claims when your property is found wanting and has caused a serious risk to your tenants' lives!

bonus tip

Being an accredited landlord carries with it the benefits of access to training courses, receiving regular updates and getting access to current information and good practice. Registering with the National Residential Landlords Association (www.nrla.co.uk) and your own local council scheme, will allow you the majority of local and national benefits. You can also use your accreditation as a marketing tool to communicate your commitment to high standards to tenants, and if necessary access personal support and advice from those organisations if you need it.

tip97

Each time you re-advertise a room, consider whether adding a few pounds per week to the price will affect its 'rentability'. In some cases, it makes the room more attractive! A few pounds difference will not affect your enquiries, but it will increase your bottom line significantly over time.

tip98

Ensure you are collecting rents on time and regularly checking them. Even a few days of late payments per month will make all the difference to your cash flow.

tip99

Keep a sharp eye on your outgoings – and take time to identify how you can reduce your bills on a regular basis. Reducing bills, even by 5–10% per annum will compound your cash flow and profits. If bills are rising fast you need to investigate and identify why. There are a number of devices available that allow you to control the heating and temperature (often the largest jump in bills is due to additional heating). Does your cleaner need to come weekly or could fortnightly be enough? Are there appliances that could be linked up to a coin operated meter and cover the cost of use? [Tumble dryers are a common culprit for rising electricity bills].

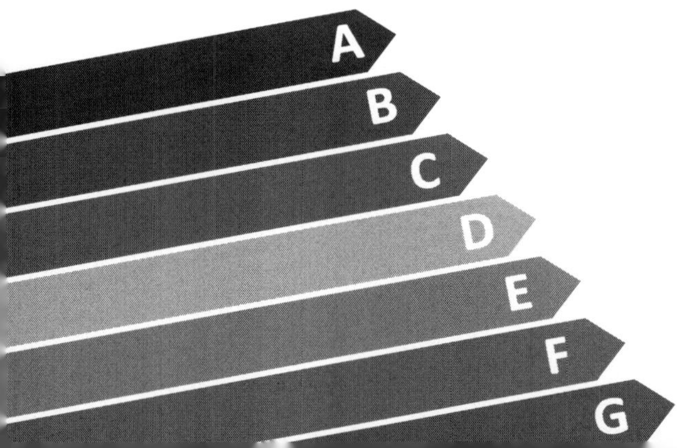

tip 100

Keep an eye on new technological developments in the HMO industry. Whether it is a new piece of software that can help notify you of late rent payments, or an app that can control your heating remotely – use technology to systemise your business, thus saving you time and money.

tip 101

And finally, enjoy your investment! You have worked seriously hard to create a property that will serve you now and for years to come, so look after it and it will look after you! Spend some of your profits, re-invest some, and never forget that your HMO should not be a High Maintenance Operation. If you implement the ideas in this book systematically and deliberately, you will soon have a flourishing HMO business which will be a Huge Moneymaking Opportunity, bringing you more time, more money and more freedom.

131
Honeywall

Article 4 Directions

"In April 2010 the Government introduced legislation that changed the planning law, and created a new Use Class of 'C4' or House in Multiple Occupation (before April 2010 small HMOs fell within the 'C3' or Dwelling House Use Class). This change required all landlords to gain planning permission before they could let what was a formerly used as a family house (C3) as a small HMO (C4) housing between three and six unrelated sharers. This is known as a 'Change in Use'. Where an Article 4 Direction is in effect, a local authority may not demand a fee for associated planning applications.

In October 2010 the Coalition Government amended the legislation. To do this, they included a 'Change in Use' from C3 to C4 within the General Permitted Development Order (GPDO). This allowed landlords to change their properties from a C3 Dwelling House to a C4 HMO without the need for planning permission. However, they also gave local authorities the power to remove permission for the C3 – C4 'Change in Use' by means of an 'Article 4 Direction'. Councils have used this to designate whole areas and limit the number of HMO's in a geographical area. The impact of Article 4 Directions Article 4 Directions are used by local authorities to limit the number of HMOs in a geographical area, for example a maximum of 10% of housing to be HMOs within a council ward.

The introduction of Article 4 applies to all HMOs in an area, it does not prevent a landlord from renting to a family, but the landlord will need to register the property as an HMO".

For more information please visit:
www.landlords.org.uk/news-campaigns

Role Description

Lead Responsible Tenant

Responsibilities

1. Waste

- To ensure bins are put out for collection on the right day
- To return bins to the property, off the pavement, after emptying
- To report to the council any missing or unemptied bins
- To report to the Landlord any issues with bins or waste
- To ensure kitchen bins are regularly emptied and deposited in correct external bins

2. Lighting

- To replace bulbs in light fittings in communal areas when the bulb has blown
- To report to landlord when stocks of light bulbs are low OR organise payment from tenants to replace lightbulbs for communal areas
- To note when a bulb has been replaced and record this

3. Security

- To report to landlord any breaches in security – i.e. front door left unlocked, windows or doors left open when tenants are out

4. Appliances

- To ensure fridge/ freezer temperature is correct and able to drain freely from back of appliance
- Check the build up of debris and ice to ensure this is not blocking fridge drains inside.
- Ensure the drain is cleaned out monthly on the washing machine
- Clean the fluff trap in the tumble dryer and empty the water condensing drawer.
- Empty the vacuum cleaner from time to time

5. Meter Readings

- To provide these on the first day of every month

Remuneration
£15 per month

Best Nest Ltd **Role Description** **Lead Responsible Tenant** **July 2015**

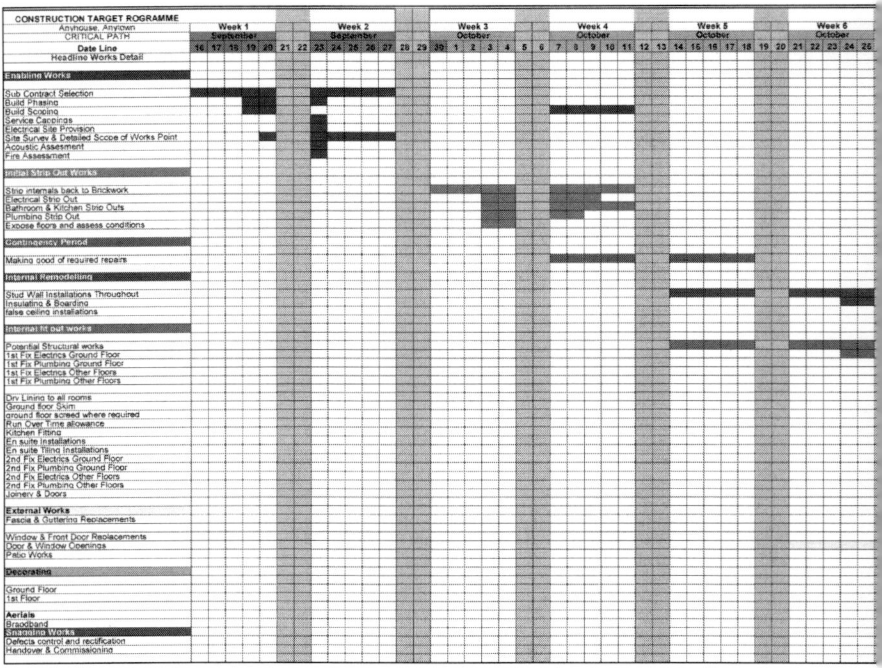
CONSTRUCTION TARGET ROGRAMME
Anyhouse, Anytown
CRITICAL PATH
Date Line
Headline Works Detail
Week 1
September
Week 2
September
Week 3
October
Week 4
October
Week 5
October
Week 6
October
16 17 18 19 20 21 22 23 24 25 26 27 28 29 30 1 2 3 4 5 6 7 8 9 10 11 12 13 14 15 16 17 18 19 20 21 22 23 24 25
Enabling Works
Sub Contract Selection
Build Phasing
Build Scoping
Service Cappings
Electrical Site Provision
Site Survey & Detailed Scope of Works Point
Acoustic Assesment
Fire Assessment
Strip internals back to Brickwork
Electrical Strip Out
Bathroom & Kitchen Strip Outs
Plumbing Strip Out
Expose floors and assess conditions
Contingency Period
Making good of required repairs
Internal Remodelling
Stud Wall Installations Throughout
Insulating & Boarding
false ceiling installations
Internal fit out works
Potential Structural works
1st Fix Electrics Ground Floor
1st Fix Plumbing Ground Floor
1st Fix Electrics Other Floors
1st Fix Plumbing Other Floors
Dry Lining to all rooms
Ground floor Skim
ground floor screed where required
Run Over Time allowance
Kitchen Fitting
En suite Installations
En suite Tiling Installations
2nd Fix Electrics Ground Floor
2nd Fix Plumbing Ground Floor
2nd Fix Electrics Other Floors
2nd Fix Plumbing Other Floors
Joinery & Doors
External Works
Fascia & Guttering Replacements
Window & Front Door Replacements
Door & Window Openings
Patio Works
Decorating
Ground Floor
1st Floor
Aerials
Braodband
Snagging Works
Defects control and rectification
Handover & Commissioning

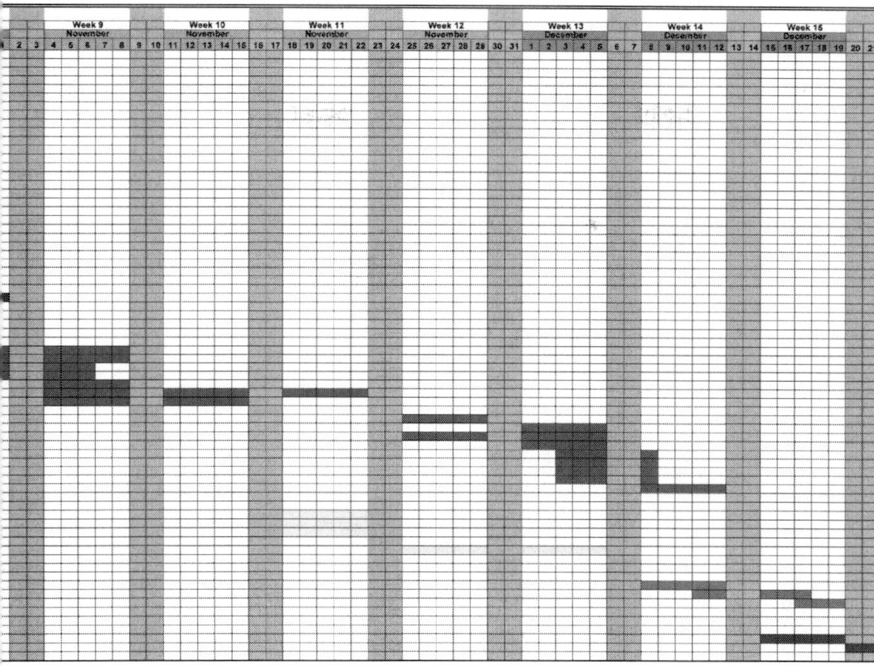
Week 9
November
Week 10
November
Week 11
November
Week 12
November
Week 13
December
Week 14
December
Week 15
December
2 3 4 5 6 7 8 9 10 11 12 13 14 15 16 17 18 19 20 21 22 23 24 25 26 27 28 29 30 31 1 2 3 4 5 6 7 8 9 10 11 12 13 14 15 16 17 18 19 20 21

BUILDING SPECIFICATION AND PLANS

Property Address	**95 Anywhere Road, Anytown**
Summary of works	**Conversion of 5 bed student HMO into a 6 bed HMO.**
Main Contractor	

Owner and Project Manager	Wendy Whittaker-Large	Tel	Email
Owner	Mark Rogers	Telephone	Email
Architect			
Building Regulations			

DESCRIPTION OF WORKS (SUMMARY)

- Install additional wiring (lighting and sockets) and move aerial points as per room data sheets.
- Install two ensuites to first floor rooms 4 & 5
- Build additional stud partition wall to downstairs room 2
- Upgrade current bathroom to modern shower room
- Install additional velux window to attic room.
- Build downstairs single storey extension to kitchen which will be extension to current kitchen plus bedroom 3 with ensuite. To be built in accordance with plan. Flat roof pitch as per plan.
- Block off existing kitchen back door.
- New kitchen to be installed
- Decorate and paint throughout with new carpets.
- Correct damp issues in small basement room
- Complete all repointing as needed
- Assess current fire alarm system & lights in cellar to confirm they conform to fire safety standards
- Assess current central heating system
- Masterkey system to be installed to all bedroom doors
- Boxing in of boiler to upstairs large shower room.

BUILDING REGULATIONS ITEMS

- Single storey extension to back of house as per plan. Using steel (xx) plan.
- Addition of 2 en-suite bathrooms on first floor
- Velux window addition to loft room.
- Stud partition wall with fireboard to make bed 2 downstairs

HMO REGULATIONS ITEMS

- Thumb turn knobs on all internal doors, as well as new front door and patio doors.
- All openings onto communal passageways to be FD30

BUILDING WORKS

- Build partition stud wall to create corridor of no less than 800 mm in downstairs bedroom 2
- Box in soil pipe from upstairs through ceiling of bedroom 2 to rear. Fill with acoustic insulation.
- Fit FD30 fire door to bedroom 2 as per room data sheets comparable with doors already in situ
- Treat damp in small cellar room
- Install new Velux window in attic space
- Create 2 ensuites in bedrooms 4 & 5 upstairs
- Additional skirting as required
- Replace plastic corrugated cellar window shield at front of house with clear Perspex shield
- Skim ceilings where required (room data sheets) or re-board especially beds 1, 2 & 4.
- Replace kitchen ceiling and add new downlighters.
- Create boxed-in cupboard for router in hallway
- Box in pipes where identified

ROOF

- Chimney pots require vented covers
- Chimney flashings to be repaired
- Guttering at rear requires replacement and repair

WINDOWS and DOORS EXTERNAL

- Fire safe exit Window to be installed in bedroom 3 (rear extension) and French doors to the new extension.
- Must have FENSA certification.
- White internal window handles.
- Specification to be agreed prior to purchase.
- Internal Thumb turn door locks on patio and front door with Masterkey system.

PLUMBING

- Plumbing for washing machine and tumble dryer in kitchen as per kitchen plan
- Shower in shared bathroom to be thermostatic from boiler.
- Sanitary ware to be agreed prior to purchase – allow mid range specification (shower screen and fixings, shower tray 800x 800, close coupled wc and cistern – short projection if necessary, wash hand basin and tap, 1 x towel radiator)
- Please allow services from new en-suites to run out to rear of building and into stack (boxing in as per above)
- Tile out 3 en-suites, 1 wc and 1 x bathroom (walls and floors) as per plan.
- Controlled wired heating thermostat

PLASTERING AND TILING

- Tiles (up to £20 sq metre) and tile fitting – bathrooms walls and floors as well as kitchen wall (part) and kitchen floor as per design specification

KITCHEN

- Kitchen up to £2,500 allowance and fitting – specification to be agreed and ordered via Contractor.

CARPETS

- Carpets to all 6 bedrooms and stairs & upstairs landing up to £10 per square metre. Carpet to be agreed prior to purchase.

ACOUSTIC BOARDING and INSULATION

- Acoustic insulation to connecting partition wall between shower rooms
- Acoustic insulation and boarding to boxing in of soil pipe in bedroom 2

ELECTRICS

- Aerial points in all bedrooms and kitchen.
- Chase cables into walls where possible
- Pendant light in all bedrooms. Strip light in cellar.
- White fittings for all points
- Must have Part P certification and inspection report for all works completed.
- Hard wired smoke alarms with 10 year warranty in all bedrooms and cellar. Heat detector in the kitchen.
- Assess whether current fire control panel working & meets regulations to BS5839 Part 4.
- Emergency lighting to be fitted per room data sheets. Emergency lighting log book and completion certificate to be provided.
- External emergency lighting to include PIR detector at back of house. Placement to be agreed.
- Minimum 3 double power sockets in all bedrooms.
- Low energy bulbs and low energy LEDs in all light fittings.
- Wireless Broadband will be installed.

INTERNAL FITTINGS

- Bedroom doors (2 and 3) to have Yale locks with internal thumb screw turn.
- Kitchen units, tops and fitted accessories specification to be agreed.

PAINTING and DECORATING

- Completely redecorate the whole house.
- Existing skirtings, picture rails and other features to be continued around new en-suites.

- All skirtings, picture rails etc – white gloss (Gliddens or equivalent)
- Ceiling matt white. (Gliddens or equivalent)
- Walls matt magnolia undercoat and overcoat with matt Gliddens "Honeysuckle White"
- White gloss fire doors (if not pre-finished to white gloss).
- Finish required to a high standard.
- Plaster sanded especially where any defects found especially in corners, on joins etc.
- All bare wood, mouldings and existing painted wood be sanded.
- Where moulding are damaged or channels made please repair / fill / replace as best to original shape.
- All imperfections, small holes, nail holes be filled and sanded.
- Caulk all ceiling, door and skirting joints twice.

LANDSCAPING

- Clear out rubbish
- Replace gravel and infill with new
- Tidy front garden and infill new gravel

PROJECT REPORTING

- Project meetings at least weekly.
- Agreed payment schedule on submission of invoice.
- 2.5% retention for snagging.
- Contractor liaison with CPR for building regulations sign-off before and after each stage.

SPECIAL COMMENTS

1. Work to be carried out to HMO regulations. Liaison required with CPR and Architect to ensure regulations are met.

2. All original features to be preserved wherever possible.

3. Existing Minton Floor in downstairs Hallway to be protected.

4. Rear of property to be secured as a priority adding new lock / bolt

5. Contractor to notify HSE before work starts and comply with HSE requirements.

6. Contractor to comply with CIS regulations.

Wendy Whittaker-Large

13.2.14

Finding It

Building regs – http://www.planningportal.gov.uk/buildingregulations/
Land registry – www.gov.uk/government/organisations/land-registry
Planning portal – http://www.planningportal.gov.uk/
Homestamp – http://homestamp.com/
www.Rightmove.co.uk
www.zoopla.co.uk
www.home.co.uk

Funding It

www.Property 118.com

VAT notice: Buildings and construction, HMRC, 2014
www.gov.uk/government/publications/vat-notice-708-buildings-and-construction708:
www.fca.org.uk

Finishing It

HMO regulations:
www.gov.uk/government/publications/licensing-of-houses-in-multiple-occupation-in-england-a-guide-for-landlords-and-managers
www.legislation.gov.uk/uksi/2006/372/pdfs/uksi_20060372_en.pdf

Lacors Guide to Fire Safety:
www.rla.org.uk/docs/LACORSFSguideApril62009.PDF

Landlords National Property Group – www.lnpg.co.uk Tel: 01455 234499

Masterkey – www.holdfast.co.uk
Holdfast Security Systems – Tel : 01270 505902

Dunelm Mill – www.dunelm.com
The Range – www.therange.co.uk
Asda – www.asda.com
BHS – www.bhs.co.uk

Wilkinsons – www.wilko.com
Loft Interiors – www.loft-interiors.co.uk
Free Phone 0800 157 7322
Email info@loft-interiors.co.uk

Japanese knotweed – www.japaneseknotweed.co.uk
(I hope you never need this one)!
Green deal – www.gov.uk/green-deal-energy-saving-measures/overview
Broadband Speedchecker – www.broadbandspeedchecker.co.uk
Julian Maurice Interiors – www.julianmaurice.com

Filling It

Landlord Law – www.landlordlaw.co.uk
Cudasign – www.cudasign.com
Easyroommate – uk.easyroommate.com
Spare room – www.spareroom.co.uk
Open Rent – www.openrent.co.uk

Future-Proofing It

Mail chimp – www.mailchimp.com
Survey monkey – www.surveymonkey.com
Mighty text – www.mightytext.net
Residential Landlords Association – www.rla.co.uk
Telephone : 0161 962 0010
Telephone : 03330 142998 (Local rate on landline and mobile networks)
Email: info@rla.org.uk

National Landlords Association – http://www.landlords.org.uk/
020 7840 8900 email: info@landlords.org.uk

www.landlordzone.co.uk
Property Tribes – www.propertytribes.com
Progressive Property – www.progressiveproperty.co.uk
PIN – www.propertyinvestorsnetwork.co.uk